THE COMMANDO POCKET MANUAL

1940-1945

Compiled and Introduced by
Christopher Westhorp

CONWAY

BLOOMSBURY

LONDON • NEW DELHI • NEW YORK • SYDNEY

Conway
An imprint of Bloomsbury Publishing Plc

50 Bedford Square   1385 Broadway
London   New York
WC1B 3DP   NY 10018
UK   USA

www.bloomsbury.com

CONWAY™ is a trademark and imprint of Bloomsbury Publishing Plc

First published by Conway 2012
First Bloomsbury edition 2015

Compilation and introduction © Christopher Westhorp 2012
Volume © Bloomsbury 2015

British Library Cataloguing-in-Publication Data
A catalogue record for this book is available from the British Library.

ISBN: HB: 978-1-8448-6159-0
          ePub: 978-1-8448-6197-2

Printed and bound in Great Britain by CPI Group (UK) Ltd, Croydon CR0 4YY

Bloomsbury Publishing Plc makes every effort to ensure that the papers used in the
manufacture of our books are natural, recyclable products made from wood grown in
well-managed forests. Our manufacturing processes conform to the environmental
regulations of the country of origin.

To find out more about our authors and books visit www.bloomsbury.com. Here you
will find extracts, author interviews, details of forthcoming events and the option to
sign up for our newsletters.

Publisher's Note
In this facsimile edition, references to material not included from the original in the
selected extract have been removed to avoid confusion, unless they are an integral part
of the sentence. In these instances the note [not included here] has been added.

CONTENTS

CHAP.   PAGE

Introduction 4

1 Commando Training Instruction No. 1, 1940...............................16
2 Notes on Training of Commandos, 1941.....................................20
  Weapon Training: Bayonet
3 Offensive Demolitions: Lochailort Fieldcraft Course, 1941............22
  Lecture 4: The Scope of Explosives
4 All-in Fighting, 1942 28
  Chapter 3: Holds
5 Shooting to Live with the One-hand Gun, 1942............................41
  Chapter IV: Advanced Methods
6 Commando Training, 1942 51
7 Combined Operations Pamphlet No. 27:.....................................67
  Hardening of Commando Troops for Warfare, 1944
8 Combined Operations Pamphlet No. 24: Cliff Assaults, 1945 89
  Section 7 – Cliff Climbing Methods and Drills
9 Notes from Theatres of War No. 11: 101
  Destruction of a German Battery by No. 4 Commando
  During the Dieppe Raid, 1943, Introduction and Parts 1-4
10 Small Arms Training: The Thompson Machine Carbine, 1942 ...119
  Introduction and Lessons 1 & 2

Index 126

INTRODUCTION

Opinions vary about the real military value and importance of the Commandos during the Second World War. However, there is less dispute that the combative Commando way – a comparatively small group of action-orientated soldiers who were determined to 'have a go' and attack the enemy whenever and wherever they could – struck a real chord with the embattled British public from 1940 onwards, earning the unit enduring heroic status.

This book will not attempt to survey the operational record of the Commandos, or to assess in any detail their organisational history or their contribution to the broader war. Instead, what follows is a selection of authentic documents that provides an interesting insight into the thinking behind the Commando concept. Detailed training programme lecture notes, an analytical after-action report and excerpts from manuals reveal how the Commando fighting spirit was cultivated and maintained, what some of the key aspects of Commando work actually entailed, and how well the training and equipment worked when put into practice.

REGAINING THE INITIATIVE

In 1940, following the evacuation of the British Expeditionary Force from Dunkirk, Britain stood alone as the last power in western Europe not to have fallen to Hitler's armies. At that crucial moment of national weakness and uncertainty, while preparations were made to resist the German invasion that was expected to follow, Prime Minister Winston Churchill was concerned that Britain should avoid becoming overly defensive-minded. Instead, in a reflection of his own pugnacious spirit, he demanded an unconventional force that would be active rather than passive in the face of an impending enemy attack. Churchill wanted troops who could harry the Axis forces, striking fear into the German occupiers of Europe. Such actions would enable Britain to regain the initiative while conventional military rebuilding continued, until such a time as a large-scale amphibious assault of the European mainland could be attempted.

THE 'HAND OF STEEL' EVOLVES

Although units of elite troops are, of course, as old as warfare itself, many military theorists in the decades before the Second World War had been developing ideas for small-scale, specialised formations and the examples of T.E. Lawrence's campaign in the Middle East, and the insurgency of the Irish Republican Army in 1919–21 had demonstrated the potential of small units trained in guerrilla warfare tactics.

Within days of Churchill's call, staff officer Lieutenant Colonel Dudley Clarke produced a proposal for independent aggressive light infantry units. His immediate inspiration was the Boer *kommando*, the irregular groups of hardy, horse-mounted frontiersmen who had used their tactical mobility and initiative to harass and tie-down larger British Army units. Clarke therefore proposed the name 'Commandos' and Churchill, a veteran of the war in South Africa, approved. Senior military figures preferred to refer to the 'Special Service'. (Not until 1941, long after training had begun, did the War Office announce that the Special Service Units – SSUs – would be called Commandos.)

In early 1940 the War Office had approved the formation of 10 Independent Companies, raised from among the Territorial Army (TA) volunteers. These men were trained in amphibious landings and fieldcraft in preparation for their involvement in Finland, but in March 1940 that campaign came to an end. A few months later Clarke was entrusted with an ad hoc department – M.O.9 – of the War Office and asked to raise a Special Service Brigade force with which to stage attacks across the Channel. No. 11 Independent Company (sometimes referred to as No. 11 Commando) provided the initial means for him to realise his idea of mobile raiding and reconnaissance, and in late June that first raid (Operation Collar) took place against four target beaches in northern France. 'Commando Training Instruction No. 1', in Chapter 1, produced in August 1940, set out some of the martial qualities and skills that it was felt volunteers would need to fulfil the new role. How effective these raids were to be as a psychological weapon was confirmed just a few months later when, in October 1940, Hitler issued his notorious *Kommandobefehl*, instructing that any captured 'sabotage troops' would be 'slaughtered to the last man' even if they were unarmed and had surrendered.

Churchill's attachment to the morale boosting, hit-and-run aspect of Commando operations may actually have been quite short-lived. The full-scale invasion of mainland Europe was the ultimate objective and from early on it was believed that Commando capability should combine the best elements of each of the three fighting services (land, sea and air). The tri-service Combined Operations Command (COC) had been set up in 1940, under Admiral of the Fleet Sir Roger Keyes, to plan and execute amphibious warfare missions against the enemy, which reflected the fact that any operation would require at least two of the services to cooperate effectively.

'SPECIAL' FORCES

Over time, the Commandos would prove to be capable of carrying out deep-penetration sabotage missions as well as acting in a spearhead or reconnaissance capacity ahead of a larger, regular formation – what would eventually be required at D-Day, and bloodily rehearsed during the Dieppe raid in 1942 (when, in a supporting action, No. 4 Commando provided a model attack on a gun battery).

As a military formation, the first ten Commandos (each one subdivided into ten troops and sections) helped to constitute the five battalions of the Special Service Brigade (SSB), with more than 5,000 men overall. In 1942 the Royal Marines organised Commando units and No.10 (Inter-Allied) Commando was formed, recruited from various European nationalities (including troops made up by Belgians, Dutch, French, Yugoslavs and Poles). In 1943, to reflect the belief that the Commandos would mostly be fighting alongside regular formations, most of the Army Commandos were unified into four SSBs in which they were combined with the reorganised Royal Marine Commando battalions. Three Army Commandos (Nos. 12, 14 and 62) remained independent, to be used for small-scale raids, but by the end of 1943 their men had been absorbed into the four SSBs, which later became Commando brigades. At the end of the war all the Army Commandos were disbanded and the Commando role was assumed by the Royal Marines.

Some of the Commandos also had sub-units; for example, No. 6 Commando had a special section known as 101 Troop that trained with Folboat canoes to carry out raids. Other specialist canoeists were trained for small operations in the Colonel Robert Laycock-inspired Combined Operations Assault Pilotage Parties (COPPs) to infiltrate enemy-held territory on reconnaissance and intelligence-gathering missions.

Commando operations encompassed both audacious, one-off attacks and lengthy campaigns, resulting by 1945 in the achievement of 38 battle honours, emblazoned on the Commando flag displayed in Westminster Abbey. The larger raids ranged from Lofoten and Vaagso (both 1941) in Scandinavia to St Nazaire and Dieppe in France. The Commandos also fought with distinction in the Western Desert and Middle East, in North Africa and Sicily, and in the Far East. Overall, between 24/25 June 1940 and 29 April 1945, the Commandos participated in approximately 145 operations.

As a consequence of being an aggressive assault unit that tried to accomplish difficult tasks, casualty rates were sometimes high and more than 1,700 Commandos died in action. The decorations awarded are testament to the valour displayed: 8 Victoria Crosses (6 posthumously), 39 Distinguished Service Orders, 162 Military Crosses, 218 Military Medals and 32 Distinguished Conduct Medals – as well as countless Bars.

RECRUITMENT

When recruiting began in 1940, volunteers ('for special service') were sought from fully trained soldiers in the existing British Army regiments, as well as the aforementioned Independent Companies, which were being disbanded. Inter-regimental competitiveness between the volunteers helped to raise the performance and requirement levels, which were highly exacting and only the very best – about 400 men – were picked by the selectors to undergo specialised training.

Churchill had urged his countrymen 'in war, resolution; in defeat, defiance …', and those were two of the qualities that were needed in the new formations. In fact, a certain type of man was expected to provide the best type of recruit to the new units; one of ideal or extraordinary character

– bright, motivated, tough, daring, disciplined, self-reliant, with an independent frame of mind. Trainers wanted Commando units to thrive on leadership rather than command. First-rate physical fitness was, of course, crucial because of the need to move fast while carrying a heavy load of equipment across all manner of difficult terrain.

Unlike regular soldiers, Commandos didn't live in communal barracks, isolated from the civilian world. They received a subsistence allowance and were expected to use their initiative to arrange accommodation, food, civilian clothing and suchlike for themselves. The creators of this revolutionary regime believed that this left the men with more time for pure operational training work, as well as doing much to nurture creative thought, independent action and self-reliance – much better than being regular soldiers drilled to obey orders and conform to a regimen. The Commando's world was soldiering of a different order, in which he provided for himself by any means necessary, including foraging to supplement rations. When Commandos found themselves in perilous and unforeseen situations, they would need to combine truculence with ingenuity.

A HARD SCHOOLING

An individual Commando had to become accustomed to the sea and at least the rudiments of seamanship – some men, of course, became more specialised in a canoeist role (most famously, the Southsea-based Royal Marines' Boom Patrol Detachment, more popularly known as the 'Cockleshell Heroes'). It was also expected that he would be confident fighting on his own or in a small group, and not just as part of the larger Commando. He had to be proficient in the use of small arms and explosives, and still feel comfortable fighting in a built-up area. Also, darkness was a Commando's friend – he had to attain a high degree of night-time effectiveness and to perfect close-up, silent killing. One senior officer even argued in a memo that bayonet proficiency was the most important element in Commando training (see Chapter 2). Irrespective of the comparative value of specific elements of the programme, the daring and difficult missions envisaged for Commandos required the most gruelling training that could be devised.

Selection and training at the outset were quite ad hoc, reflecting the independent nature of some of the units. Gradually, however, a more centralised and structured programme was developed to achieve a measure of uniformity. In order to rehearse Commando methods of warfare, places were needed where recruits could be pushed to the limits in suitably wild and unforgiving terrain, far from prying eyes, and before long one particular part of the UK proved to be the ideal schooling ground – Lochaber in the western Highlands of Scotland.

One of the first instructors was a native of the area, Simon Fraser – better known as the 17th Lord Lovat, chief of the Clan Fraser, who helped to establish an all-forces special training centre at Lochailort, with an adjunct at Achnacarry, and there were others at Knoydart, Arisaig and Moidart. The Independent Companies had set up at Achdalieu in 1940, and that September the COC established a shore establishment at Inverary, where about 250,000 Allied personnel eventually learned about small landing craft amphibious warfare (and the Commandos learned seaborne assault). All the deer forests from Achnacarry to Knoydart in the far west were requisitioned to provide several hundred thousand acres in which to train.

From 1942 onwards Achnacarry became the main centre for Commando instruction after the chief of clan Cameron allowed the British military to use Achnacarry Castle, the ancestral seat of Cameron of Lochiel, to establish the Commando Training Depot (later the Commando Basic Training Centre). After they had completed their six-week training course, which quickly earned a reputation as the most arduous training centre within the entire Allied Forces network, volunteers were posted to their Commando units. The commandant (1942–5), Lieutenant Colonel Charles E. Vaughan, reported to Combined Operations headquarters in London. Vaughan, convinced that it is 'all in the mind and heart', believed passionately that his instructors impart to each Commando a will to keep going regardless of the adversity encountered. 'Commando training' entered the military lexicon, meaning, to borrow David Stirling's phrase, the 'unrelenting pursuit of excellence'. During those several years about 25,000 soldiers – British, Canadian, American, French and Dutch, among others – underwent their stamina-stretching schooling at Achnacarry, which they affectionately called

'Castle Commando', and earned the right to wear their green beret.

Achnacarry was organised into several training Commandos and the tuition followed a carefully prepared syllabus with all the specific skills that were crucial to raiding. Recruits learned and were rigorously tested, by day and by night (in all weathers), in physical fitness, outdoor survival training and living off the land, fieldcraft (the art of moving across country unnoticed and unheard), rope work and 'Tarzan' courses, the skilled handling of various weapons (including enemy small arms), unarmed and close-quarter combat (including silent killing), map-reading and compass work, signalling, explosives and demolition skills, rock-climbing, amphibious and cliff assaults, small boat operations, river-crossings, first aid, marksmanship and live-fire training. For a body of soldiers expected to infiltrate enemy-held territory and sabotage the infrastructure, being able to use high explosives was a particularly important capability. The extract presented in Chapter 3 dates from March 1941 and is part of a series of six lectures spread over 22 hours that was given at Lochailort, devoted to the subject of offensive demolitions.

The technique of unarmed combat was then quite original. Indeed, it could be argued that close combat generally was *the* specialism that defined the Commandos – a symbol of their tenacious fighting spirit. This new art was created by William E. Fairbairn and Eric Anthony Sykes, whose policing experiences in crime-ridden Shanghai had made them experts in pistol shooting and all manner of ungentlemanly techniques, including hand-to-hand combat and knife fighting. The men invented a close-quarters combat system for British military instructors, which both the Commandos and Special Operations Executive (SOE) learned as part of a course that Sykes formalised into Silent Killing, to be taught at Lochailort (and later Achnacarry). Writing in *All-in Fighting* in 1942, Fairbairn observed, 'In war, your attack can have only two possible objects: either to kill your opponent or to capture him alive'. Chapter 3 of the same book details a number of effective holds, by means of which a sentry might be overcome, and this is reproduced here in Chapter 4. Sykes's expertise in small arms, which he wrote about in the influential *Shooting to Live* (1942), was also put to use in teaching the Commando instructors innovative combat pistol techniques. The section on Advanced Methods makes up Chapter 5.

The single-minded focus of the dedicated instructors at Achnacarry was to turn out the finest and fittest fighting man in a month and a half – professionals who could follow an order, but who were also intelligent and able enough to use their own initiative. Yet for all its unconventionality, Achnacarry did not lack the traditional military idea of order. Vaughan was of the opinion that, 'A man who keeps his equipment clean, no matter the conditions under which he is living, will also keep his body and mind tidy and alert'. This point was echoed in a fascinating paper prepared by Lieutenant Colonel Laycock in January 1942 and presented in Chapter 6. Posing important questions about the direction Commando training should take, and offering some answers, Laycock's conclusion stressed the crucial importance of training being absolutely thorough.

Speed has always been a key virtue in warfare. More than a century earlier Wellington had accepted that he needed swift, light, picked troops for specific tasks, and the Commandos, operating as non-mechanised troops in a fast-moving warfare environment, accentuated the need to move fast on the battlefield. At Achnacarry the trainees would speed-march in battle order, carrying all their weaponry and equipment, 7 miles uphill to Spean Bridge, then negotiate an assault course while having to apply accurate weapons' fire. In training, one troop marched 63 miles in less than a day, having covered the first 33 miles in eight hours; another troop, in field service order and carrying five days' supply, marched 130 miles. Such marches, it was declared in *Combined Operations Pamphlet No. 27* in 1944, 'are the rule, not the exception'. Although highly trained modern athletes now know the value of a scientific approach to conditioning, similar guidance was issued to the Commandos more than half a century ago. The pamphlet, produced in Chapter 7, was based on lectures given by Surgeon Commander G. Murray Levick, RN, who had several years' experience at the special training centres, offering observations on the hardening of the body and the science of rationing.

Climbing was included at Achnacarry, but in December 1942 a dedicated Commando Mountain Warfare Training Centre was set up at

Braemar in the Cairngorms. It was subsequently decided not to use Commandos in this role and mountain training was later moved to St Ives where the role changed to audacious cliff-assault training in preparation for D-Day. A short section from *Cliff Assaults*, 1945, on 'Cliff Climbing Methods and Drills' is reprinted in Chapter 8.

OPERATIONS

Although the prime minister turned out to be hostile to what he dismissed as 'pinprick raids', he still wanted the Commandos to evolve their raiding concept. Therefore, in October 1941, following Keyes's replacement by Lord Louis Mountbatten, one of the first missions he authorised was Operation Archery, a hazardous amphibious assault by No. 3 Commando, supported by men from No. 2, on the Nazi-occupied Norwegian port of Vaagso. The Commandos lost 17 men, but killed about 150 of the enemy and took 102 prisoner. The Vaagso raid also signalled that the role of the Commandos could be expanded further to shock assault brigade, holding a bridgehead, providing cover for a landing in force, and suchlike.

In March 1942 the Commandos raided St Nazaire (Operation Chariot). The objective was to try to deter the German battleship *Tirpitz* from Atlantic waters by putting out of action the only dry dock that was capable of holding her for repair. The operation was a costly one for the Commandos, yet it was successful. The dry dock was never used.

Less than six months after the triumph at St Nazaire, an even costlier attack was made against the German defences at Dieppe (Operation Jubilee). The Allied force of about 6,000 men included more than a thousand Commandos acting in a support capacity. During a subsidiary operation, No.4 Commando provided what was hailed as a 'classic example of the use of well trained infantry' in destroying a gun battery near Varengeville. An after-action analysis by the War Office is reprinted in Chapter 9. The Dieppe mission has long been categorised as a disaster, but in recent years historians have painted a more favourable picture, though both interpretations largely agree that the value lay in the lessons learned then applied in June 1944 during the D-Day landings in Normandy.

EQUIPMENT

Throughout the war most of the principal weapons of the Commandos were the same as those used by British infantry – for example, the Boys anti-tank rifle, the PIAT anti-tank weapon and the Bren light machine gun. Not as accurate as the Bren, but capable of greater rates of fire, was the belt-fed Vickers 'K' gun, which was adopted later in the war by the Commandos. Because Commando units had to be comparatively small but powerful, they tended to focus on automatic weapons and ordnance. Despite the fact that he was often acting as a light infantryman, each Commando often carried a huge amount of equipment into action and he trained to do so over a distance. Other items of equipment favoured by the Commandos include silenced firearms and rocket grapnel cliff-scaling tools, but a few weapons in particular have become widely recognised symbols, notably the 0.45-inch calibre Thompson sub-machine gun and the fighting knife.

In an important night raid, it might be necessary to eliminate key sentries in such a way that the alarm could not be raised. The quietest way to do this was to jump the sentry from behind and use a dagger. The instructors of unarmed combat at Lochailort, captains Fairbairn and Sykes, collaborated with Wilkinson Sword to design the iconic, well-balanced Commando knife that bears their names, the FS Fighting Knife. The double-edged, razor-sharp tapered blade was long, slim and sharp-tipped enough to slip through the human ribcage. The training programme at Achnacarry ensured Commandos knew how to inflict fatal wounds that could bring death in as little as three seconds.

Specialist missions often needed tailor-made equipment. The Commandos and the agents of the SOE, similarly tasked with 'setting Europe ablaze', had a shared need for unique tools to accomplish specific jobs – such as a quiet, compact, accurate firearm capable of killing at a reasonable distance. Both groups used the Welrod silenced pistol and the Welgun light sub-machine gun that was supplanted by the Sten MkIIS (or suppressed Sten), but the best special mission weapon was a modified hybrid of Lee Enfield rifle, Thompson sub-machine gun barrel and Colt pistol magazine, with a highly effective suppressor designed in 1942 by British engineer William de Lisle. An order for 500 de Lisle carbines (.45-inch calibre) was placed, but only around 150 ever came into use in the British military, nearly all of them with the Commandos.

The standard pistol and sub-machine guns of the Commandos throughout the war were the .45-inch Colt automatic and the Thompson M1928A1, or 'Tommy gun', described in the British Army's 1944 edition of the Small Arms Manual as 'a weapon of opportunity ... eminently suitable for patrols and street fighting'. The Thompson sub-machine gun was first produced in 1938, and after the British Army had witnessed the effect of sub-machine guns on the Allied armies in 1940, it ordered more than 100,000. The early deliveries went predominantly to Commando units, where it was loved for its powerful punch and reliability. From 1942 a simplified version, the M1, was introduced. The official training pamphlet, a sizeable extract of which is reproduced in Chapter 10, provided instructions on handling, loading and unloading, holding and firing, and stripping and cleaning.

The .303-inch, magazine-fed Bren light machine gun provided an ideal support weapon, which was put to devastating effect on the first major Commando raid against Vaagso in December 1941 – testament to the esteem in which this weapon was held is the fact that it was used (converted to 7.62 millimetre) in the 1991 Gulf War.

ENDURINGLY SPECIAL

Born out of a position of weakness, the creation and actions of the Commandos prepared the ground for what was eventually a success story. Combined Operations Command described their 'amphibious guerrilla warfare' as something to which the British were: '... by temperament and tradition, peculiarly suited. The national love for the sea could be combined with the national love of the chase...' Goebbels dismissed them as 'Red Indian' raids, yet the Native American was a fierce and implacable foe – a peerless warrior in his chosen terrain. Throughout the modern world, 'Commando' indicates a military elite of carefully selected soldiers who have met high standards of training, and physical and mental toughness. The template of that excellence and courage was laid down during the Second World War by the British Commando units.

Although the Army Commandos were disbanded at the war's end, the term 'Special Service' persisted. Today, more than 70 years after the Second World War began, the Commando legacy lives on in the Royal Marines and three other British military units widely acknowledged to be among the very best of their kind – the Special Air Service (SAS), the Special Boat Service (SBS) and the Parachute Regiment – which can trace their origins and ethos to the decisions made in 1940 to form the Commando units. As military legacies go, that ranks among the best.

CHAPTER 1

COMMANDO TRAINING INSTRUCTION NO. 1

**The War Office
15 August, 1940.**

1.   The object is to train a guerrilla force, organized in units equivalent in strength to a weak battalion (500 men), and to operate independently in "smash and grab" raiding operations into enemy territory.

Raids carried out by commandos will normally be planned to last not longer than 24 hours actually spent in enemy territory, and not more than one commando is expected to be employed in any one operation.

2.   For operational purposes it is intended that the commando organization should be as loose as possible, each troop, and individual soldier, being trained to work independently—prepared if necessary to rely entirely on their own resources both operationally and administratively in any circumstances which may arise.

The commando will often be operating over a wide area in small groups which must depend upon their speed and cunning to avoid action with organized enemy forces. These groups must be prepared to seize every advantage and opportunity to achieve their object and inflict damage on the enemy. In short, their task will be to strike suddenly and get away again before being brought to action.

The creation of such a force calls for the highest standards of training, personal and collective discipline, courage, skill, determination and imagination in all ranks—backed up by inspired leadership and organizing ability on the part of their commanders.

Training will therefore aim at producing: —

(a) A very highly developed team spirit and *esprit de corps*;

(b) Self-reliance and resourcefulness on the part of each individual.

It is the greatest mistake to suppose that these two aims are incompatible, and every commando leader must foster a collective spirit as well as a spirit of individualism in his commando.

3.   Training will differ from that normally given to the regular soldier in that the greatest stress must be laid on the ability of each man to decide his own course of action without being told what to do. A common and, in some ways, justifiable criticism of Regular Army training is that the men are marched everywhere and every detail of their lives is organized and prepared for them, so that the men do not learn to look after themselves. This is to some extent caused by the necessity for economy in time and the fact that administrative centralization is necessary to keep maintenance costs down. On the other hand, this "herding together" of the men does allow a close supervision of their daily lives and enables a high standard of discipline (which is absolutely necessary in any form of warfare) to be enforced. If this supervision is relaxed it is clear that an even higher standard of individual discipline must be insisted on.

It is, therefore, most essential that any methods adopted to encourage self-reliance and independence shall not at the same time produce a feeling of irresponsibility which will certainly lead to failure on active operations.

4.   Individual training should be designed to instil the following qualities: —

(a) *Esprit de Corps.* "A pride in the show" should be fostered by insistence on very high standards of turnout, bearing, saluting, punctuality, care of arms, and physical fitness.

(b) *The Offensive Spirit.* The men must be taught that their object is the destruction of the enemy and that they must "get their man" at all costs, regardless of what is going on around them.

They must, therefore, attain a very high degree of skill at arms, both by day and night, and be prepared to use any weapon which may be given to them or which may fall into their hands.

As offensive raiding will almost certainly include sabotage, instruction should also include simple means of destroying such enemy material as:—

> Petrol stocks,
>
> M.T. vehicles (including A.F.Vs.),
>
> Aircraft,
>
> Guns,
>
> Railway signal boxes,

and, if possible, the vital points of power stations and aerodromes. The stalking of isolated enemy posts must also be practised.

(c) *Silence and Secrecy*. It is essential that the soldiers shall be taught not to give away the fact that they are training for a special task and the nature of that task. This particularly applies to soldiers going on leave, who may be tempted to discuss their activities with their families.

(d) *Self-Reliance*. This includes the ability of the man to look after himself under all conditions, and to be able to find his way by day and night without the assistance of a section leader or an officer.

Men must be trained in map reading and fieldcraft and be taught to develop night sense and a hunter's cunning.

(e) *Inquisitiveness*. Soldiers must be taught that, although it is their first duty to carry out their primary task, yet they must not allow any opportunity to slip of acquiring fresh information which will be of value.

(f) *Opportunism*. The men must be ready to take advantage of any equipment or transport which can be seized during a raid, and they must be able to drive any normal type of car or lorry. They must be ready to obtain information from the enemy, including enemy casualties, and must always try to turn circumstances to their own advantage.

(g) *Open-mindedness*. Unfamiliar and unexpected conditions must be accepted as part of the day's work. Transport may be by sea or air and men must be ready to swim or move in small boats. Training in watermanship is therefore necessary.

(h) *Physical fitness*. All forms of physical training will be of value, including swimming with and without lifebelts and with and without weapons, boxing, and, if possible, ju-jitsu.

(i) *Intelligence.* A man's intelligence may usefully be developed by making him memorize written or verbal instructions, directing special attention to getting the intention behind any orders received. Training should also be given in making reports, both written and verbal.

(j) *Miscellaneous.* What to do if taken prisoner. Normal training in stalking, concealment, camouflage, and silent movement over all types of ground.

5. Collective training will be designed to give instruction in the various stages of a raiding operation, such as: —

(a) Embarkation: stowage of weapons and stores; rapid disembarkation and trans-shipment to smaller craft at sea.

(b) Disembarkation on to beaches, including landing from smaller warships and, if possible, submarines.

(c) Movement from and withdrawal to beaches individually, or through other troops, and collective withdrawal from close contact with the enemy.

(d) Attacks on aerodromes, railway junctions, power stations, etc.

(e) Attacks on headquarters, hotels, billets, etc., with a view to capturing prisoners and documents.

(f) Creation of diversions in connection with more regular forms of warfare.

(g) Street fighting and rioting.

(h) Terror tactics among disorganized enemy troops and civilians.

(i) Emplaning and deplaning.

Prepared under the direction of
the Chief of the Imperial General Staff.

(B40/373) 150 8/40 W.O.P. 5982

CHAPTER 2

NOTES ON TRAINING OF COMMANDOS.

12 May 1941.

WEAPON TRAINING.

BAYONET.

Though under present day training principles the bayonet has taken rather 2nd. or even 3rd. place, in special training for Commandos or any other type of assault troops it should take precedence over all other weapons. There are 3 reasons for this (The 3 "Ps" Psychological, Physical, Practical.)

1. Psychological.

Nothing can so much develop the offensive spirit so necessary to special units as the bayonet. The average Englishman needs mentally toughening for the somewhat drastic actions demanded of Commando soldiers. The idea of it being a matter of satisfaction to "stick" your enemy can only be developed by progressive training in bayonet until the man likes his bayonet as a weapon and the idea of using it in actions. This will never be done by the rather dreary "On Guard" "High Port" "Pass Through" Routine. Varying practices must be introduced.

Training Method. Once the on guard position has been taught and a good point developed (Men should know this on arrival at Commando Training Establishments) work on the standing and lying sacks should be started. Then the Butt under and over taught and practised. As realistic as possible "Final Assault Course" With at least six targets should be constructed and be the next stage in training. Instructors must avoid a mere mechanical performance and keep the squad on its toes. "Dirty Tricks" such as kicking should be taught and encouraged for use on the dummies. Training should never be stressed to boredom; but returned to from time to time. A periodical run down the assault course can be given in short training periods.

2. Physical.
Bayonet practice of judiciously employed over short periods at "Full Stretch" is excellent physical as well as mental training.

Training Methods. Vary runs down the assault course. Give with bullet and without. Unfix bayonets and attack with "Butt, Boot, and Bullet". Always keep a squad on its toes with surprise orders, etc;

3. Practical.
The vital importance of hand to hand weapons in typical Commando work cannot be too much stressed. In night raiding fire should be avoided as much as possible. Experience in schemes and in operations has shown, especially at night, that fire is nearly always opened too soon and often on another party of our own troops (Fondness for the bayonet would do much to mitigate this) in the confusion of the "Dog Fight" which is likely to occur, the bullet is as dangerous to ones own side as to the enemy. The deadly vicious silence of a surprise attack with the bayonet only would have a tremendous moral effect on the enemy, besides confusing him as to the position and intentions of his attackers.

Summing up.
Proficiency in the use of, and a desire to use the bayonet; is most important to all troops especially to the type of troops we are training. Experience has shown that even men who consider the bayonet as a boring form of physical drill, can be made keen and efficient with careful and varied training.

CHAPTER 3

OFFENSIVE DEMOLITIONS

Lochailort Fieldcraft Course
March 1941.

LECTURE 4

THE SCOPE OF EXPLOSIVES.

1. Quick destruction.

We said at the beginning of the course that our object was to teach you to destroy things quickly. We have now shown you how to use explosives and incendiary, and how either may be combined with booby mechanisms and time delays. Let us now see how explosives can be used for the destruction of certain actual objectives.

A modern army may march on its stomach, but it certainly does so along a road. Good communications are more vital than ever to the present-day highly mechanised army. The needs of its stomach – food, petrol, ammunition – can often be destroyed by fire, but communications – roads, railways – can only be effectively destroyed by explosives. Let us see how to attack them.

2. Bridges

As bridges are common to both roads and railways, let us consider them first.

A bridge may be either a simple, single span or else it may have more than one span resting on **piers** in the middle. Speaking generally, there are three ways of attacking it.

(a) Cut the bridge itself in two.

(b) Upset the end of the bridge by a mined charge in the **abutment.** (The abutment is the bit of firm ground that the bridge rests on at each end.)

(c) Cut the pier so that the bridge collapses by its own weight.

One, or any combination of these methods may be used. (b) is seldom effective alone. Let us now take the different types of bridge in turn.

Simple Girder Bridge. A typical small railway bridge with sleepers resting on I – girders. Cut the bridge one third from the home side – the home side because it's harder for the enemy to climb up the steep side than drop down it. Cut each girder, the side pieces, the rails, the handrails, and anything else that may help to hold the bridge up. Cut them on a slant, so that the heavier part of the bridge can drop away from the rest without jamming.

You will require something of the order of 100 lbs. of explosive and two hours preparation to fix the charges.

Trussed Girder Bridges. A typical large railway bridge with a criss-crossed system of angle irons and tie rods. Cut the bridge as before, on a slant, one third across.

You will require something of the order of 200 lbs. of explosive and four hours preparation.

Arch Bridge. A typical secondary bridge, with brick, stone, or concrete arch. If the arch is very flat indeed and the bridge new-looking, it may be reinforced concrete. If so, leave it alone.

The centre of the bridge is called the **crown**, and the side parts between the crown and the abutments the **haunches**. The strength of the bridge is in the arch itself, which is usually only say 1′ 6″ thick; all the rest above it is just filling. It is easy to dig through the filling and then you have only the thickness of the arch to cut. (Break up the road surface with a small charge first). The best place to cut the bridge is at the haunch, but then you have to dig more than at the crown. Lay the charge right across the bridge and up the side walls or **parapets**. If you cannot dig away the filling, you have to add all that onto the thickness to be cut.

Alternatively mine the abutment – 50 lbs. 5 feet in, but you will probably require two or three charges to cover the whole width. Again you have to dig, or use the successive charge method in from the side.

You will need something like 100 lbs. of explosive, digging tools and 4 hours preparation.

Suspension Bridges. A typical bridge in mountainous country. Again cut the bridge, cutting everything across it, including the stiffening girder under the roadway, but as the bridge will flop both sides, cut it anywhere, at the easiest place. Remember to use scissor charges on the cables.

You may need only 50 lbs. and one hours work.

Viaducts, or any Bridges with High Piers. Cut the pier, laying your charge all along one side of it, if possible a few feet above the bottom.

You will require up to 1,000 lbs. but only two hours preparation.

Reinforced Concrete. Any flat concrete bridge is reinforced, – typical modern first class road bridges. These bridges are too difficult for you to attempt, unless you have over 1,000 lbs. of explosive and have nothing better to do with it, in which case heap it all in the middle of the bridge and hope for the best.

3. Roads.

It is difficult to make a complete block against say medium tanks, but effective temporary blocks can be made as follows:

Culverts. Or drains running under the road on a hillside. Put a mined charge or charges in the culvert – 50 lbs. 5 feet in, more if it is deeper, and you probably require two to cover the whole width of the road. The charge must be tamped, and this takes time. Use earth or stones with blankets, pillows, curtains etc. from the nearest house to help.

Say 100lbs. 2 hours.

Retaining Walls. Where the road runs along a steep hillside. Break into the wall by successive charges and lay mined charge to blow away the road. Say 100 lbs, 2 hours.

Buildings. Bring down houses where the road is narrow through a village street. Use a concussion charge in the appropriate rooms.

Say 50 lbs. per room, half an hour.

Rocks. In mountainous country fall rocks onto the road – but this is seldom worth it, as the rocks are often easy to clear away, and are apt to overshoot the road. But if the strata is right, put a well tamped charge of say 5 lbs. in a crack behind each suitable charge.

Trees. Fell trees across the road. Say 10 lbs. per tree and 15 minutes to fix each charge.

4. Railways.

Railways are easy and lend themselves particularly well to booby traps.

Miles of track can be destroyed by cutting a rail every 200 yards with one slab of explosive very quickly fixed in place (rubber bands). A gap of 200 yards between each demolition makes repair a lengthy job as it is too far to carry a new rail easily, so the repair van has to move along each time. A few hidden pressure switches and a few A.P. bullets will add to the difficulties.

Or wreck a train, especially in a tunnel, with pressure switches or fog signals. This is usually better than destroying the tunnel itself, which is nearly always very strong.

5. Lock Gates

Lock gates are best destroyed at the hinges. Best of all, put a mined charge in the bank behind the hinge, but a quick method is to lower a charge (50 lbs.) down to the bottom on the upstream side against the hinge.

6. Other demolitions.

There are many other varied objectives for demolition work. Piers and jetties can be destroyed by cutting the piles or supports, pylons and dock cranes can be overturned by cutting the legs. Each case is different, but always decide whether to use a cutting, mined or concussion charge and lay it accordingly.

7. Organisation.

A successful demolition requires a carefully prepared plan. A good reconnaissance is invaluable, and may enable you to prepare the charge beforehand. Think of the tools, stores, transport and working party you will require, and of the local protection while doing the work. Have a rendezvous before the work, and a rally point after it. Lastly, make a simple and very definite arrangement about the order to fire the charge.

8. Strategy.

In offence, demolitions will be most useful in a raid and this is probably your most likely use of them. The whole of the next lecture is devoted to that.

In defence, in a rapid withdrawal, demolitions are your best weapon. You will seldom have the time or the explosive to make a complete obstacle, but this need not dismay you, though it should be your aim. Indeed the enemy is prepared for the bridges to be blown and may be bringing new ones up already made to fit. But he is not prepared to find a small obstacle, a tree felled here, a retaining wall or culvert blown there, round every corner of the road, each covered by fire and complicated booby traps. Small demolitions, each well within your power, in great depth, are of inestimable value.

PRACTICAL 4

PLACING CHARGES

1.   Work in two squads, "A" and "B", "A" being twice the size of "B". One officer instructor in charge, and one N.C.O. instructor with each squad.

2.   Both squads inspect **Concrete Railway Bridge**, and decide on method of demolition and charge required. (5 mins).
    Points to bring out:–
    (a) Neither arch nor pier reinforced concrete (Why?).
    (b) Pier quickest and easiest place to attack. Cut it right across.
    (c) Average thickness 50″, therefore 7 lbs. per 6″ of width. Width is 40 ft., therefore total charge 560 lbs.
    (d) Lay charge along groove cut in ground – particular case where other side is unsupported and groove gives tamping.
    (e) For speed, lay charge in its boxes with primer in each, and short cordtex lead coming out of each. Then use ring main, with each short lead knotted to it with a clove hitch. Result, one gun cotton or T.N.T. box per foot, or one row of boxes all along. This method is bad if any space is left between the boxes and the pier, but take the wooden slats off the boxes and the tamping should enable you to make close contact. Each box with its short length of cordtex may be prepared beforehand.

(f) Party, say 10 men. Time, say ½ hour if boxes are already prepared.

(g) Borehole method, requiring tools and about a day's work, would only require charge of 36 lbs.

3. Squad "A".

Move to **Red Bridge** and lay gun cotton and P.E. cutting charge. One student to be in charge of work under instructor's guidance. Girders, rails and handrails to be cut. Cordtex ring main to be used. Dummy detonators.

4. Squad "B".

Move to Camp Bridge and lay T.N.T. and P.E. cutting charge. Student in charge, Cordtex ring main, dummy detonators.

5.   Half an hour from end of period, squads change over, and inspect and dismantle each other's work.

6. Transport.

One truck to be allotted to take stores to and from bridges, and to transport students.

7. Stores Required.

	At Red Bridge:	At Camp Bridge:
Gun Cotton	28 lbs.	
T.N.T.		14 lbs.
Dummy P.E.	10 lbs	10 lbs.
Primers	30	20
Dummy Detonators	2	2
Cordtex, odd lengths	150 ft.	100 ft.
Safety Fuse	24 ft.	24 ft.
Adhesive Tape	4 reels	2 reels
Strong	1 ball	1 ball
Hand Axe	1	1

CHAPTER 4

ALL-IN FIGHTING

by W.E. Fairbairn, 1942.

CHAPTER 3. HOLDS
NO. 12. THUMB HOLD

This is the most effective hold known, and very little exertion on your part (three to four pounds' pressure) is required to make even the most powerful prisoner obey you. It is possible also for you to conduct him, even if resisting, as far as he is able to walk. You have such complete control of him that you can, if necessary, use him as cover against attack from others.

The movements you have to make to secure this hold are very complicated, which is mainly the reason why it is almost unknown outside of the Far East. But the advantage one gains in knowing that one can effectively apply this hold more than repays for the time that must be spent in mastering it.

Students should first concentrate on making every move slowly, gradually speeding up, until all movements become one continuous motion. When they have thoroughly mastered it, as demonstrated, they should then learn to obtain it from any position in which they have secured their opponent.

Students must also understand that the hold is not a method of attack, but simply a 'mastering hold', which is only applied after they have partially disabled or brought their opponent to a submissive frame of mind by one of the 'follow up' methods (Blows).

Should your opponent not be wearing a tin hat or similar protection which covers his ears, the following will be found to be a very simple method of making him submissive:

Cup your hands and strike your opponent simultaneously over both ears, as in Fig. 41. This will probably burst one or both ear drums and at least give him a mild form of concussion. It can be applied from the front or from behind.

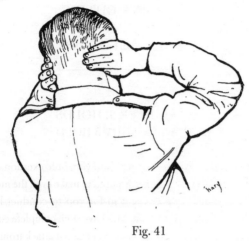

Fig. 41

Stand facing your opponent and slightly to his left.

1. Insert your right thumb between the thumb and forefinger of his left hand, your fingers under the palm of his hand, your thumb to the right (Fig. 42).

2. Seize his left elbow with your left hand, knuckles to the right, and thumb outside and close to your own forefingers (Fig. 43).

3. Step in towards your opponent; at the same time, turn your body so that you are facing in the same direction, simultaneously forcing his left forearm up across his chest and towards his left shoulder by pulling his elbow with your left hand over your right forearm and forcing upwards with your right hand (Fig. 44).

It will be noted that you have released the hold with your left hand, which was done immediately his elbow was pulled over your right forearm. Also that your opponent's left elbow is held very close to your body.

4. Keeping a firm grip on the upper part of his left arm with your right

arm, immediately seize the fingers of his left hand with your right. This will prevent him from trying to seize one of the fingers of your right hand and also give you an extra leverage for applying pressure as follows:

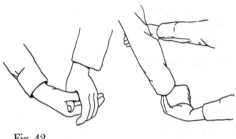

Fig. 42   Fig. 43

Press down on the back of his hand towards your left-hand side with your right hand. Should your opponent be a very powerful man and try to resist, a little extra pressure applied by pulling his fingers downwards towards your left-hand side with your left hand will be sufficient to bring him up on his toes and convince him that he has met his master (Fig. 45).

Fig. 44   Fig. 45

NO. 13. SENTRY HOLD

The success or otherwise of any attempt to carry out this method of attack on a sentry will, apart from the fact that you have thoroughly mastered every movement, depend entirely on every possible condition having been taken into account. It would, to say the least, be very inadvisable to take it for granted that the sentry would be standing in a certain manner or that he would be wearing his equipment (gas mask, pouches, or rifle, etc.) in the orthodox manner.

It is taken for granted that the attack will be applied from behind; the stalk or approach to the sentry will be during the hours of dark or semi-dark; the sentry has been under observation for a sufficient length of time to permit of his habits (length of his post, position of his rifle, if carried, and his normal halting or resting position) being known; and that the man selected for the attack is an *expert at stalking*.

Now let us assume that conditions are somewhat on the following lines:

1. Rifle slung or carried on the right shoulder.

2. Wearing a steel helmet covering the back of the neck and the ears.

3. Wearing a respirator on the small of his back, projecting as much as six inches (See Fig. 46).

Fig. 46

4. There are other sentries within shouting distance.

It will be admitted that these conditions are not too favourable for the attacker, but are what might have to be met, and students are advised to carry out their training under conditions as near as possible to those they will have to contend with in actual war.

Note.—The stalker should not be handicapped with any equipment, other than a knife or a pistol. He should wear rubber or cloth shoes, socks pulled well up over the trousers, cap-comforter, well pulled down with the collar of his blouse turned up and his hands and face camouflaged (See Fig. 47).

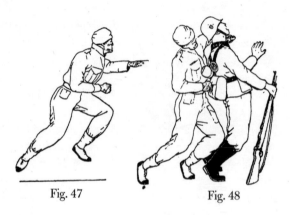

Fig. 47   Fig. 48

1. Having approached the sentry from behind to within three to four feet, take up position shown in Fig. 47. This will permit you to make a lightning-like attack by springing on him.

2. With the fingers and thumb of your left hand fully extended, *strike* him across the throat with the inner edge of your left forearm (i.e. with the forearm bone), and simultaneously *punch* him with your clenched right hand in the small of his back or on his respirator case (Fig. 48).

The effect of these blows, if applied as above, will be that you have rendered your opponent unconscious or semi-conscious. Further, it should be noticed that the blow on the throat will cause your opponent to draw his breath, making it impossible for him to shout and give the alarm.

3. The blows should be immediately followed with a very fast movement of your right hand from the small of his back, over his right shoulder, clapping it over his mouth and nose (Fig. 49). This will prevent him from breathing or making a noise in the event of the blow on the throat not having been effectively applied.

It is not unlikely that the blows on the throat and in the small of the back may cause him to drop his rifle or knock his helmet off his head. Should this happen, no attempt should be made to prevent them falling on the ground. Just simply keep still for a matter of ten seconds, after which it is unlikely that anyone having heard the noise will come to investigate.

Fig. 49

Retaining your hold around the neck with your left arm, drag him away backwards.

Note.—To enable students to form some idea of how effective this method is when applied as above, and so that they will also have confidence that it can be successfully used by a man of normal strength, we advise them to have it applied on themselves by a friend, care being taken that no more than one-twentieth of the normal force is used.

NO. 14. JAPANESE STRANGLE

1. Approach your opponent from behind.

2. Place your left arm round his neck, with your forearm bone bearing on his Adam's apple.

3. Place the back of your right arm (above the elbow) on his right shoulder and clasp your right biceps with your left hand.

4. Place your right hand on the back of his head.

5. Pull him backwards with your left forearm and press his head forward with your right hand, and strangle him (Fig. 50).

Fig. 50

Note.—Should your opponent attempt to seize you by the testicles:

(a) Keep your grip with both arms, straightening out the fingers and thumbs of both hands. With the edge of your left hand in the bend of your right arm, place the edge of your right hand just below the base of the skull.

(b) Step back quickly, at the same time jolting his head forward with the edge of your right hand, and dislocate his neck (Fig. 51).

(c) In the event of your opponent being a taller man than yourself, making it difficult for you to reach his right shoulder with your right arm, as in Fig. 50, bend him backwards by applying pressure on his neck with your left arm. If necessary, punch him in the small of the back, as shown in Fig. 48, Sentry Hold, and bring him down to your own height.

Fig. 51

NO. 14(A). JAPANESE STRANGLE APPLIED FROM IN FRONT

1. Stand facing your opponent.

2. Seize his right shoulder with your left hand and his left shoulder with your right hand.

3. Simultaneously push with your left hand (retaining the hold) and pull towards you with your right hand, turning your opponent completely round (Fig. 52). It should be noted that your left arm will be in a position around his neck and most likely you will have caused your opponent to have crossed his legs, making it almost impossible for him to defend himself.

4. Place the back of your right arm (above the elbow) on his right shoulder and clasp your right biceps with your left hand.

5. Grasp the back of his head with your right hand, and apply pressure by pulling him backwards with your left forearm and pressing his head forward with your right arm (Fig. 50).

Note.—Although the final position and the method of applying pressure are identical with that shown in No. 14 on the previous page, there is a difference in the amount of pressure necessary to strangle your opponent. If his legs are crossed (and they nearly always will be, when he is suddenly twisted round in this manner), approximately only half the amount of pressure is required.

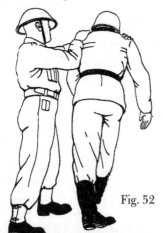

Fig. 52

Fig. 50

NO. 15. HANDCUFF HOLD

1. You are facing your opponent. Make a dive at his right wrist, seizing it with both hands, right above left, jerking it violently downwards, as in Fig. 53. This will produce a considerable shock, amounting almost to a knockout blow on the left side of his head.

2. Swing his arm up to the height of your shoulder, at the same time twisting his arm towards you so as to force him off-balance on to his left leg (Fig. 54).

Fig. 53   Fig. 54

3. Keeping his arm the height of his shoulder, pass quickly underneath by taking a pace forward with your right foot. (It may be necessary for you to reduce your height to permit of your doing this; do so by bending your legs at the knees). Turn inwards towards your opponent, jerking his arm downwards, as in Fig. 55.

4. Step to his back with your left foot, and with a circular upward motion, force his wrist well up his back. Retain the grip with your left hand and seize his right elbow with your right hand, forcing it well up his back. Then slide your left hand around his wrist, bringing your thumb inside and finger over the back of the hand, and bend his wrist. Apply pressure with both hands until your opponent's right shoulder points to the ground (Fig. 56).

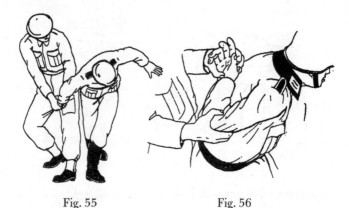

Fig. 55   Fig. 56

Note A.—This is a very useful hold for marching your prisoner a short distance only.

Note B.—A method of tying up your prisoner is shown on page 86, method A [not included here].

NO. 16. BENT ARM HOLD

Note.—Students are strongly recommended to specialize in mastering this hold.

1. Your opponent has taken up a boxing stance or raised his right arm, as if about to deliver a blow.

2. Seize his right wrist with your left hand, bending his arm at the elbow, towards him (Fig. 57). Continue the pressure on his wrist until his arm is in the position shown in Fig. 58.

These movements must be continuous, and carried out as quickly as possible. It will be noted that forcing your opponent's right forearm backwards places him off-balance, making it almost impossible for him to attack you with his left fist.

3. Immediately step in with your right foot, placing your right leg and hip close in to your opponent's thigh.

4. Pass your right arm under the upper part of his right arm, seizing his right wrist with your right hand above your left.

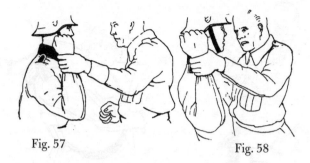

Fig. 57

Fig. 58

5. Keeping a firm grip with both hands, force his right elbow and arm against your chest, applying pressure by jerking his wrist towards the ground. At the same time, force the forearm bone of your right arm up and in to the back muscles of the upper part of his right arm (Fig. 59).

6. Should your opponent, when in this position, attempt to strike you with his left hand, straighten out the fingers and thumb of your right hand, placing the edge of the hand over your left wrist, and apply the pressure by a sudden jerk upwards of your right forearm, taking care to keep his elbow well in to your chest (Fig. 60).

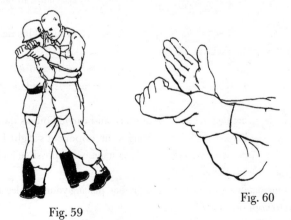

Fig. 60

Fig. 59

NO. 17. HEAD HOLD

Approach your opponent from the front.

1. Keeping the finger of your right hand straight and thumb extended, strike him on the left side of his neck with the inside of your right forearm (Fig. 61). This blow will render your opponent 'punch-drunk' or dazed.

2. Immediately after delivering the blow with the forearm, slide it around your opponent's neck, simultaneously stepping across his front with your right leg, bending him forward from the waist and catching hold of your right wrist with your left hand (Fig. 62).

3. Force your right forearm bone into the right side of his face—(anywhere between the temple and the chin will do)—by pulling on your right wrist with your left hand and forcing downwards on the left side of his face with your body.

It should be noted that the outside of your right forearm is resting on your right thigh and that the weight of your body is being forced on to your right leg by pressure from the left foot. Any attempt of your opponent to seize your testicles should immediately be countered by a slight increase of pressure. If necessary, apply an edge of hand blow—release your hold with the left hand, straighten up slightly, and apply the blow on the left side of his neck.

Fig. 61

Fig. 62

CHAPTER 5

SHOOTING TO LIVE WITH THE ONE-HAND GUN

by W.E. Fairbairn and E.A. Sykes, 1942.

CHAPTER IV
TRAINING: ADVANCED METHODS

Chapter III has taken care of all the stages of the recruit's preliminary training, but before he is turned loose on the world as qualified to use a pistol there is one more thing for him to learn. This is shooting from what, for want of a better term, we call the "three-quarter hip" position illustrated in Fig. 12.

Fig. 12.— "Three-quarter Hip" Position

This position is designed to meet a condition referred to in the first chapter when describing the circumstances under which shooting affrays are likely to take place. We indicate there that in moments of stress and haste men are apt to fire with a bent arm.

Examination of the illustration shows exactly this position. Closer examination shows also that the firer is facing his adversary squarely, has one foot forward (it docs not matter which), and that he is crouching slightly.

From this position, pistol hand in the vertical centre-line of the body and hand bent to the right as before, the recruit fires a burst of two or three shots, but *quickly*, at a distance of 3 yards. If he succeeds in making nothing worse than a 6-inch group, he should repeat the practice at 4 yards.

The instructor should make a special point of explaining all the elements of this practice. The bent arm position is used because that would be instinctive at close quarters in a hurry. The square stance, with one foot forward, is precisely the attitude in which the recruit is most likely to be if he had to fire suddenly while he was on the move. The "crouch," besides being instinctive when expecting to be fired at, merits a little further explanation.

Its introduction into this training system originates from an incident which took place in 1927. A raiding party of fifteen men, operating before daybreak, had to force an entrance to a house occupied by a gang of criminals. The only approach to the house was through a particularly narrow alley, and it was expected momentarily that the criminals would open fire. On returning down the alley in daylight after the raid was over, the men encountered, much to their surprise, a series of stout wires stretched at intervals across the alley at about face height. The entire party had to duck to get under the wires, but no one had any recollection of either stooping under or running into them when approaching the house in the darkness. Enquiries were made at once, only to reveal that the wires had been there over a week and that they were used for the wholly innocent purpose of hanging up newly dyed skeins of wool to dry. The enquiries did not, therefore, confirm the suspicions that had been aroused, but they did serve to demonstrate conclusively and usefully that every single man of the raiding party, when momentarily expecting to be fired at, must have crouched considerably in the first swift traverse of the alley. Since that time, men trained in the methods of this book have not only been permitted to crouch but have been encouraged to do so.

The qualification we require before the recruit's course can be successfully passed is 50 per cent. of hits anywhere on the man-sized targets employed. Time has shown this to be adequate for the purpose in view.

We indicate elsewhere our aversion to trophies, badges, etc. No "expert's" or "marksman's" badges are issued to men who pass our recruit or other courses, no matter how much in excess of 50 per cent. their scores may have been. If a man makes "possibles" throughout, his only reward is the resultant confidence in himself and the satisfaction of knowing that if he has to "shoot it out" with a pistol he will be a better man than his opponent.

Similarly, we have a dislike of "team shoots." We feel that the ammunition would be much more usefully employed in giving additional practice under instruction.

From now on, in proceeding to more advanced training, the use of stationary targets should be abandoned in favour of surprise targets of all kinds and in frequently varied positions. Such targets would include charging, retreating, bobbing, and traversing figures of man-size. Traversing targets can be either at right or oblique angles. Musketry officers will have no difficulty in devising for themselves endless variations on this theme, and current incidents, more especially in the nature of actual happenings to men of their particular service, often provide valuable suggestions.

We will give one example of a practice which has been frequently carried out with good results. It is designed not only as a test of skill with the pistol under difficult conditions, but also a test of bodily fitness and agility, qualities which to the policeman at any rate are every bit as necessary in the circumstances which are so often encountered in shooting affrays.

In this practice, which we have called the "Pursuit," the shooter is started off at the run, outside the range, on an obstacle course consisting of jumping a ditch, running across a plank over water, crawling through a suspended barrel, climbing a rope, a ladder, and over a wall, finishing up with a 100 yards dash ending at 4 yards from the targets. Without warning or waiting, two surprise targets arc pulled, one after the other, and at each he fires a "burst" of three shots. The targets are exposed for no longer than it takes to fire three shots at the highest possible speed.

Yet another practice, a "mystery shoot," is described in the chapter entitled "A Practical Pistol Range."

In all practices at surprise targets, opportunity must be found for the performance of two very essential operations. In order of importance, these are :—

1. Making safe after firing only a portion of the contents of the magazine.

2. Inserting a second magazine after totally expending the contents of the first and continuing to fire without delay.

In the first instance, after firing one or two shots from a fully charged magazine, the instructor should give the order to cease fire. The shooter should then come to the "ready," remove the magazine, eject the live round from the breech, work the slide back and forth several times and finally pull the trigger, all as described in Figs. 9 and 10 [not included here].

In the second instance, immediately the last shot has been fired, the shooter comes to the "ready," removes the empty magazine, inserts a fresh one and reloads, either by pressing down the slide release stop with the thumb of the left hand or by slightly retracting and then releasing the slide. The slide flies forward, taking a cartridge into the breech, and the shooter resumes the "ready" position by bending his hand to the right and awaits the appearance of the next target.

Practice at surprise targets can be carried out first with the arm fully extended and later from the "three-quarter" hip position. There are still two other methods of close-quarter shooting to be described, but before doing so this will be perhaps an opportune moment to call the attention of instructors to several points which will be of assistance in getting results.

When firing at surprise targets, never let men anticipate matters by standing in the firing position. They must be standing at the "ready" before the first target appears. If the succeeding targets are pulled with no perceptible interval, the men may continue to stand in the firing position. Otherwise they should come down to the "ready" again after each shot or "burst" while awaiting the appearance of the next target.

Attention has been drawn already to the necessity for the square stance. When turning from one target to another the square stance must be preserved by turning the body. This can be effected by scraping the feet round or even jumping round if the extent of the turn warrants it. It does not matter how it is done so long as the firer faces each fresh target squarely and is thus enabled to retain the pistol in its original position, *i.e.* in alignment with the vertical centre-line of the body.

In firing at a crossing target ("running man"), it will soon be observed that 90 per cent. of all the misses are traceable to firing ahead of it or, as a man accustomed to the shot-gun would say, to "leading it." This holds good even when the range is only 4 yards and the target only travels at about 3 miles an hour. This is not the place for a controversy over the rival merits of "landing" a moving target or "swinging" with it. Our purpose is merely to assist instructors in correcting their pupils' mistakes, and we content ourselves with pointing out that, distance and speed of target being as stated, a bullet travelling at eight hundred feet a second would strike only about three-quarters of an inch behind the point of aim.

We now turn to the two other methods of close-quarters shooting previously referred to. These are, respectively:—

The "half-hip" (Fig. 13).

Fig. 13.— "Half Hip" Position

The "quarter" or "close-hip" (Fig. 14).

Fig. 14.— "Quarter" or "Close-Hip" Position

Apart from shortening the arm by bringing the elbow to the side, the "half-hip" is no different from the "three-quarter," and should be practised at not more than 3 yards. Above that distance it would be more natural to shoot from the "three-quarter" position.

The "quarter" or "close-hip" position is for purely defensive purposes and would be used only when the requirements are a very quick draw, followed by an equally quick shot at extremely close quarters, such as would be the case if a dangerous adversary were threatening to strike or grapple with you. Practise this at 1 yard. This is the only position in which the hand is not in the centre of the body.

Before we close the subject of shooting at short ranges, we would ask the reader to keep in mind that if he gets his shot off first, no matter whether it is a hit or a miss by a narrow margin, he will have an advantage of sometimes as much as two seconds over his opponent. The opponent will want time to recover his wits, and his shooting will not be as accurate as it might be.

It will be appropriate now to turn our attention to training ourselves for shooting at longer ranges, for in spite of having said that the great majority of shooting affrays take place within a distance of 4 yards, the need does arise occasionally for a long shot.

For a long shot in the standing position, we think the two-handed methods shown in Figs. 15 and 15A are best calculated to produce results.

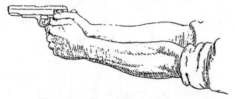

Fig. 15.— Two-Handed, Standing

The right arm is rigid and is supported by the left. Practise at any reasonable distance from 10 yards upwards.

Fig. 15A.— Two-Handed, Standing

Fig. 15 shows the proper method to employ if you have to shoot from the prone position (Fig. 16). Incidentally, do not be afraid to adopt this position immediately if circumstances demand it, as might be the case if you had to deal with several adversaries simultaneously. Practise yourself in getting quickly into the prone position, remembering that it gives you the dual advantage of being able to do your shooting from a steady position at a mark which is against the sky-line, as it were, while you yourself offer a less

Fig. 16.— Two-Handed, Prone

conspicuous target for your opponents than if you were standing up.

Kind providence has endowed us all with a lively sense of self-preservation and some of us with a sense of strategy as well. If our readers are in the latter class we need not remind them of the advantages of taking cover whenever possible. It is possible, however, that some of you have not thought of a telephone pole or electric light standard in that connection. Fig. 17 will show you a side view of how to do it most conveniently, and Fig. 18 shows how an adversary will view the matter. Note in the former illustration the position of the feet, knees and left forearm. The left knee and

Fig. 17.— Side View.

forearm are pressed against the pole, left hand is grasping the right wrist, thumb of the right hand resting against the pole. Fig. 18 also demonstrates the almost perfect cover provided.

If the long shot gives you enough time to deliberate, so much the better, because the two-handled position and that of Fig. 17 permit of almost rifle-like accuracy. But do not take it for granted that you will have time to be deliberate. It is wiser to assume that you will not, and it will be to your advantage, therefore, to practise all three of the two-handed methods at the same surprise targets as are used for short-range work.

We have condemned the use of sights for all forms of short-range shooting, but for long shots, such as we have been describing, sights offer a distinct advantage. We have little faith, however, in those usually furnished. Good as some of them are for use against a white target and a black bull's eye, there are very few that can be picked up instantly against a dark background, and this difficulty is increased to the point of being insuperable if the light is bad. To overcome this, the authors' personal pistols are fitted with foresights of silver, of exactly the shape of the ordinary shot-gun bead and about the same size. If kept bright, these sights collect any light there is from any angle and can be seen instantly in all circumstances except pitch-darkness. They stand up very well to rough work and can be easily replaced if damaged. We see no reason

Fig. 18— Front View

against the adoption of this type for service issue if some suitable white-metal alloy were used instead of silver. Though not claimed as suitable for target work, these sights answer their purpose admirably where speed is the prime consideration.

The best rear-sight for use in conjunction with the silver bead is a wide and shallow "V." The rear-sight should be affixed with a distinct slope to the rear, and once the gun is sighted-in, should be kept in place with a small set-screw. It will not shoot loose then and will be less liable to displacement or loss by accident or ill-usage.

CHAPTER 6

COMMANDO TRAINING

To G (Training), G.H.Q., M.E.F.
From Lt.-Col. R.E. Laycock.
10th January, 1942.

I. GENERAL

1. Role and organization require settlement.

It is difficult to lay down a definite policy for training Commandos until two fundamental questions have been finally settled :—

First, what is the primary role of a Commando?

Secondly, What is to be its organization?

In a comparatively short time during which I have been connected with these units, which have been described in terms as contradictory as "an undisciplined rabble" and "The Famous British Commandos" (the former by a War Office general, the latter by the German General Staff) they have varied in size between Battalions over 1,000 strong, with no less than 72 officers, to units of 18 officers and 356 O.R.s.

They have been borne on their establishment a diversity of specialists ranging from the Parachutist to the Folbotist, and have been conveyed to the theatre of operations in aircraft and in submarines, in Glen-ships and in gunboats, in 30-cwt trucks and in destroyers. They have made landings from A.L.C. and whalers, from rubber punts and R-boats, and have been called upon to carry out tasks as markedly different as a coastal raid by 50 men, to a 3-day rearguard action by the best part of a Brigade covering the withdrawal of regular infantry.

The problem of their future training is therefore not easily solved, and much of what follows will appear platitudinous to the regular soldier, the more so since I have always contended that 80% of Commando training should be conducted upon the normally accepted lines, there being little to add to the curriculum of the modern infantryman.

2. Offensive spirit. Training at night.

Two outstanding features cannot, however, be over-stressed:– The development of the offensive spirit, and the importance of training at night.

3. Initial Troubles.

It may be well to begin by enumerating some of the difficulties which arose during the "toothing period" of these units, which caused grave errors to be committed in battle, but which should now be set right by a more suitable organization and more thorough training.

4. Lack of supporting weapons and administrative organization.

The most apparent trouble of Commandos was that they were frequently employed in operations which, though initially entailing more specialized form of approach, invariably culminated in their acting in the role of ordinary Infantry. In this they found themselves handicapped by 2 factors:—

(1) They possessed no close support weapons to enable them to fight their way to objectives.

(2) They had no administrative organization for their maintenance in the field.

5. Role limited to raids.

The obvious answer is that similar operations should in future be carried out either by ordinary Infantry units who have been trained at the C.T.C., or the W.E. of Commandos must be increased to include the necessary weapons and personnel, unless their role is limited purely to raiding operations, for which they were originally raised.

6. Premium placed on discipline.

Another evil which affected a few, though not many, of the original units was a misconception of the term "toughness". A certain type of both officers and men thought they were "tough" if they looked tough, which consisted in forgetting to shave, in wearing dirty uniforms, and in demonstrating a generally low standard of discipline.

Such behaviour was severely discountenanced, and a premium placed on drill and turnout, though it was explained that the parade ground was a means to an end, and that the stereotyped formations and movements practised there should never be aped in the field. What was required was the iron discipline of the perfect soldier, which ensures that he can be relied upon to do his duty under the most desperate conditions, entirely regardless of personal considerations.

We explained that it took years to make a soldier, whereas any fool could learn to be a gangster in a few weeks.

7. The problem of specialists.

The next problem was how far the specialist should remain a separate entity, or to what extent all ranks within the commando should be trained in specialized duties. (I shall not digress upon the training of Folbotists or Parachutists, since they must obviously remain as separate units, and do not come within the scope of these notes).

The theory held by some that, since Commandos were composed of picked men, every individual could be a trained sapper and signaller as well as a rifleman and a Tommy-gunner was, I am convinced, a grave error.

Although, if practicable, this theory would have been ideal, since any sub-unit of a Commando, being self-contained, could have undertaken any task, nevertheless it remains obvious that if, for example, an operation entailing the blowing up of a bridge is to be carried out successfully, then the detachment concerned must contain a proportion of skilled sappers.

8. Sappers and signallers essential.

I therefore insisted in retaining with the Commando which I raised a specialist troop consisting of a number of R.E. personnel commanded by a regular Sapper Officer. Though they participated in normal Commando training, they concentrated on specialized work; a portion of them being allotted to other detachments as requisite for any specific operation.

A signal troop, also essential, was included in the organization of both the Home and the M.E. [Middle East] Commandos.

9. "Amateur" Sappers unsuccessful.

In addition to the above, as time and opportunity arose, we trained as many personnel as possible in elementary demolitions and in signalling. The latter proved to be of value, though the former I still believe to have been a mistake.

A "Little learning is a dangerous thing", and one cannot play at sappering. We later found ourselves forced to rely on amateur demolition parties, with the result that the success achieved on several operations was disappointing, because the demolition attempted misfired. Charges had got wet, or were not placed in the most advantageous positions; the wrong sort of explosives were used or tamping had not been thorough: circumstances which could not possibly have arisen if experts had been employed, but the like of which will occur nine times out of ten if we rely on those who have merely dabbled in technicalities.

There is, of course, no reason why the dutyman cannot operate the various types of fool-proof devices designed for specific purposes, such as the delay action explosive-cum-incendiary bomb invented by Lieut. Lewis, which has been used with such marked success for the destruction of aircraft by L Det. S.A.S. Brigade.

10. All ranks trained in S/P and morse.

An elementary knowledge of signalling, on the other hand, we found to be advantageous and all ranks, except those who were never likely to become proficient, who could be picked out in the first or second week, were trained to send and read at slow rates, using a simple procedure in both S/P and morse lamp.

Training must be thorough, and no-one who fails to classify to standard can be permitted to signal in the field, since a half-proficient signalman is an abomination.

The Signal Troop proper concentrated on W/T and R/T. There is still room for improvement in the operation of the No. 18 set, with which we were issued. We found it a temperamental instrument, upon which it was dangerous to rely.

11. Progressive training.

Commando training, like all other forms, should be progressive, and is therefore divided into individual, collective, and what might be called "Inter Service" training. These are referred to in detail later.

The ideal to be arrived at is that any detachment of fully-trained men which is ear-marked for an operation – e.g., a coastal raid – should rehearse the plan with the Royal Naval craft and personnel concerned over exactly similar approaches and ground until they are thoroughly conversant with them. They must then be made to tackle the same problem assuming that various untoward contingencies have arisen, including that of finding themselves landed at considerable distances from the selected beach.

It is most important that any troops attached for the operation should be given an early opportunity of working together with the Commando. (On the Bardia raid in April '41, the majority of a party of the R.T.R. attached for the operation were desperately seasick, whilst the remainder, having had little previous training, were physically unfit, and could not keep up with the main body in scaling the ascent from the beach).

Concert pitch should be reached just prior to sailing for the operation but, in the past, we came up against another serious difficulty to which there can be no answer until we assume and retain strategic initiative. No sooner had the required standard of training been reached than the operation was cancelled, and it is significant that we have never yet carried out a single project for which extensive rehearsals have been conducted, although many others have been mounted at short notice without adequate preparation.

Continued promises of action which culminated in cancellation had a noticeable effect on morale. The men lost interest, and it became more difficult on each occasion to explain that the prospective operation had been postponed, but that new ones were contemplated. Any race-horse trainer would have been horrified by our methods (those best calculated to produce "staleness") and, on looking back, it might possibly have been wiser to have accepted a more level tempo, though we naturally desired to sail at concert pitch, in the same way that the trainer works his horse up until the day of the race. Unlike the trainer, however, we could never be certain that our horse was going to run.

The answer, so often given us, was that we were men and not horses, and that all must be prepared to wait. There are moments, however, when the soldier does not appear to be much more intelligent that the racehorse!! Luckily, the list of subjects enumerated in paragraphs 14–36 below is so long, and may be added to, that the revision of the inclusion of new or advanced aspects of the lessons laid down should leave little time for Commando personnel to develop boredom.

II. INDIVIDUAL TRAINING.

12. T.O.E.T.

Commando recruits should join the unit as fully trained soldiers. The subjects hereafter mentioned are therefore limited mainly to those which must be learnt in addition to the purely Infantry syllabus which, however, will also be continued. T.O.E.T. should be carried out; tests for those subjects not normally taught being easily improvised.

13. Eradication of the unfit.

At an early stage, those men who are found unsuitable for Commando work or who appear unlikely to "train-on" should be returned to their units. These are men who, no matter how keen, are naturally clumsy, hopelessly seasick or abysmally dull-witted. There is another type of man who, however hard he tries, can never grasp the importance of security, and whose tongue wags after a glass of beer. He, too, must go.

14. Familiarity with the elements.

As soon as possible, the individual must develop a familiarity with the sea and the air; elements which usually prove so unfriendly to the soldier.

It is therefore essential that Commando units should be stationed on the coast, where small boats are obtainable.

After initial instruction in boat-pulling, seamanship, and, if possible, in sailing, small parties of 2–4 should be allowed to take out their own boats, provided that they have passed the necessary swimming tests, wearing battle-dress and equipment.

They must always wear Mae West life-jackets, and it is as well if a motorboat with an experienced crew is standing off in case of emergency.

Later, during Inter-Service training, all must also become familiar with larger ships and with the methods and terminology of those who man them.

Flights in Troop-carrying aircraft are usually more difficult to arrange, though the more often these can be made the better, since there are many who, though quite good sailors, suffer from air-sickness on their first few flights.

15. Self-confidence and initiative: various subjects.

The next attribute required is self-confidence. The individual must be made to develop a sense of self-efficiency, and must be early broken of the habit of relying on the "normal channel of communications". He must be taught that he must not expect his rations to be delivered under the supervision of a kindly C.Q.M.S., nor can he always look for guidance to an officer or N.C.O., but must be prepared to act alone and on his own initiative.

Way-finding. He must learn to find his way by compass, and by the heavenly bodies, and to study foreign maps. He must be taught to pick out landmarks, but it must be explained that neither these nor a route he has taken will look the same when viewed from a reverse direction, and he must therefore look continually over his shoulder on an outward journey, and work out back bearings, which must be checked on his return.

Rations & cooking. He must train to exist for varying periods on short rations, and to make the best of his mess-tin, composite ration and tommy cooker.

Field-craft and use of ground concealment. Field-craft and the art of the hunter are the next to be developed and the would-be Commando expert must learn to see without being seen. He must receive training in the use of ground, in concealment and camouflage and in the use of the stalking glass, but he must bear in mind that these are only a means to an end, and are the methods by which he will achieve his objective, get to grips with the enemy and eventually make good his escape.

It is quite remarkable how long it took us to drum some of these lessons into the modern youths recruited from the large towns. They were at first reluctant to look further ahead than the length of an average block of houses, appeared never to have observed such natural phenomena as the phases of the moon, and were quite incapable of selecting concealed positions from which other definite objects could be observed: but they trained quickly, and, in my opinion eventually made the best soldiers as they were less perturbed by the noise of battle than their normally quieter country neighbours.

Messages, reports, sketches. Exercises in which men were sent out singly or in pairs to nearby towns to find out what was made at certain factories, and which machinery was vital and could be easily sabotaged, combined with the writing of reports and messages and the drawing of sketches, proved useful, and at the same time revealed regrettable gaps in the security schemes of the factories concerned.

Weapon training; P.T.; Miscellaneous subjects. During this period, much time was still allotted to Weapon Training (including training in the use of enemy weapons) and the men were kept fit by P.T., boxing and route marches; but new subjects were introduced which included M.T. driving, house-breaking, gangster methods, unarmed combat, and the use of various devices for sabotage purposes; whilst we arranged for visits and tours of inspection of aerodromes, W/T stations, Docks and factories.

Security. Lectures were given explaining the paramount importance of security, conduct in the event of becoming a Prisoner of War, enemy tactics, identification and organization and elementary foreign words and phrases. The officers were taught the procedure and practice of R/T, interpretation of air photographs, and the use of the stereoscope. All ranks learnt S/P and Morse and underwent a course in elementary demolitions.

Drill and A/G Training. A minimum of two drill parades per week were included in the programme, and the required standard of Anti-gas training was maintained.

16. Training by NIGHT all-important.

The next step forward was to teach the individual that darkness was the raider's friend and was the medium in which they would almost invariably work. Although this theme was not fully developed until later in collective and Inter-Service Training, it was introduced at an early stage, and every lesson learnt by day which could also be carried out at night was studied again during the hours of darkness.

Men were sent out alone and in small parties and learned to move about quietly, quickly and with confidence on the darkest nights. They were taught that the human voice would give away a detachment quicker than anything else, and that for the purposes of contacting their comrades on a foreign shore, practically any pre-arranged sound was permissible, save speaking in English.

From now on more and more of our training took place at night. A policy from which we have since derived considerable benefit.

III. COLLECTIVE TRAINING.

17. Inter-Unit Schemes.

Collective training speaks for itself, and little can be added to the information contained in the manuals. The lessons learnt during individual training were put into practice by the larger formations, and Inter-Troop, and eventually Inter-Commando Competitions were introduced.

18. Control.

Commanders were given an opportunity of practising the control of their sub-units, and it is worth recording that junior officers and N.C.Os. were inclined to get carried away with "gangster" ideas, and tended to forget their duty as leaders, which resulted in a very poor standard of control.

In certain units, subalterns and Sergeants were armed with Tommy guns and spent their time looking for suitable targets for themselves instead of leading their detachments. In my opinion, no-one senior to a Corporal should be allowed to touch a Tommy gun.

19. Protection.

In the excitement of raiding, many elementary lessons were forgotten. This was particularly noticeable as far as "protection" was concerned, especially during withdrawal to the beach after objectives had been attacked. Commanders failed to detail rear parties and, on arrival at R.Vs. near the beach, forgot to arrange for local protection whilst awaiting re-embarkation.

20. Interference with Junior Leaders.

Another fault was that Commanders were inclined to interfere with their own Junior Leaders once the plan had been put into operation. This resulted in confusion, and on one operation was the cause of 50 men being left in enemy territory.

21. Dress and equipment.

We continued experiments which had been started during individual training, in deciding upon the most suitable methods of wearing equipment and carrying loads. On the whole, I am sure that we still tend to sacrifice mobility by carrying too much ammunition, as I have never yet known a case in which the Commandos fired more than half their allotment in action.

The steel helmet was discarded as being heavy, noisy and clumsy, and the cap-comforter substituted.

Footwear is a more difficult problem, and must depend on conditions likely to be encountered in each specific operation. We frequently took both Army boots and rubber shoes with us, changing the former for the latter when within stalking distance of the objective. Nailed boots are wholly unsuitable for work from iron decks or on sea-weed covered rocks. Rope-soled boots are excellent, but are tiring if worn on long marches ashore, and cannot be used in the desert, where sand and small stones work up through the soles. Rubber-soled boots or shoes are preferable to any other form if real stealth near the objective is desirable, but they should not be worn on long approach marches, especially if the ground is wet after rain.

22. Further miscellaneous subjects.

Further subjects to which particular attention was paid during the early stages of Collective Training included Street Fighting, Force marches, detachments "lying-up" during daylight and operating at night, siting and construction of road-blocks and ambushes, reconnaissance and attack of opportunity objectives, and the penetration of perimeter defences of vulnerable points.

23. Speed essential.

Special emphasis was laid on the necessity for speed, particularly in the approach to objectives. We tried to imbue all ranks with the determination to complete their tasks, regardless of what was happening on their right and left, unless this ran counter to Operation Orders.

24. Obstacles: Wire.

Delays were caused through running into unforeseen obstacles. If these are not in close proximity to the enemy, a speedy reconnaissance over as wide a front as possible must be carried out by the whole detachment simultaneously, instead of adopting the sheep-like, follow-my-leader attitude which troops are inclined to favour.

Methods of dealing with wire were studied, including the use of the Bangalore Torpedo; and obstacle races, carried out at night, proved both efficacious and enjoyable.

25. Formations.

We failed to attach sufficient importance to adopting formations suitable to local conditions, and, having carried out the majority of our training on the supposition that we should raid on pitch-black nights in Europe (where the danger of losing touch necessitated moving in very close formations) we found ourselves much too "bunched up" when we first operated on a star-lit Mediterranean night.

We later adopted a loose arrow-head, well spread out, with the Commander in the centre.

26. Recognition.

The problem of Recognition is peculiarly difficult in raiding operations, particularly just after landing, and again during the withdrawal to the beach. I have already seen two British officers shot by our troops; incidents which could easily have been avoided on both occasions.

The responsibility must be a dual one. The onus of ensuring that we are recognized when rejoining our own forces lies on the Commander of the approaching detachment just as much as on the Commander of the post approached (although this does not absolve a sentry in any way from withholding his fire until satisfied of the identity of any troops nearing the position).

The problem is simplified by using dimmed, coloured electric torches for identification, in addition to the normal challenge and countersign. Any recognition signals to be used in an operation should be constantly practised on board ship during the outward passage, thus obviating the possibility of individuals failing to pay sufficient attention, and forgetting the countersign when suddenly challenged in battle.

27. Mountain Climbing: Sabotage.

During later stages, schemes were carried out in new types of country, cliff and mountain climbing were introduced, and more detailed methods of sabotage were studied. We were sometimes lucky enough to obtain captured enemy material (e.g., a derelict Me 109) with which to experiment.

At this period, all training overlapped whenever possible with Inter-Service training.

IV. INTER-SERVICE TRAINING.

28. Co-operation between the Services.

Inter-Service Training should start as soon as possible after Individual Training has been completed, since many of the early exercises can be combined with those of Collective Training.

We now aim at developing the closest possible co-operation between the Royal Navy, The Army and the R.A.F. This will never be achieved until each knows something of the other's work, and learns to appreciate the difficulties with which they are continually faced.

The soldier must understand how ships and aircraft behave, and must become conversant with the language spoken at sea and in the air; he must know the meaning of orders and the reason why they are given. At the same time, it must be explained to the Navy and the Air Force that the soldier's problem differs completely from their own, once contact with the enemy has been gained.

Detailed or technical knowledge is undesirable, and any attempt on the part of one Service to interfere in the realms of another must be severely discountenanced.

All that is required is that everyone should know what is happening and what to expect next, so that each may help rather than hinder in the execution of the joint plan.

29. Accommodation in H.M. Ships.

Every advantage will accrue from troops being accommodated as early as possible in the ships from which they will eventually operate. Officers get to know each other, and ratings and soldiers make friends after the domestic troubles of the lower deck have been overcome. These invariably arise through ignorance but are soon smoothed over. (e.g., the soldier thinks all hammocks look much alike, and is inclined to sling the first one that comes to hand, until he learns by bitter experience that it is nearly as black a crime to pinch a bluejacket's hammock as it is to sleep with his girl friend).

30. Early lessons: Boat Drill.

The first lessons to be learnt are the tactical stowage of troops and stores in landing craft, and the perfection of boat drill. Troops must go to boat stations at least 20 minutes before manning at night, to allow their eyes to become accustomed to the darkness. Material easily damaged by sea water must be stowed carefully, and watches, matches, compasses, etc., may be conveniently wrapped in Italian French-letters, a free issue of which is obtainable in the M.E.

31. The Beach.

The next lessons concern the beaches. Detachments must learn to clear them like scattered cats, since there is normally a tendency to hang about after disembarkation.

Naval Beach Officers, Military Liaison Officers and the various beach parties must be trained to work in the closest collaboration with each other and with the troops ashore. All must know the general plan and the strengths, tasks and timings of other detachments.

32. Withdrawal and Re-embarkation.

Ships must normally be given a good offing by daylight, and the time by which re-embarkation must be completed, and after which no landing craft will remain on the beaches is therefore usually laid down by the Royal Navy.

Careful training is necessary to ensure that detachments leave their objectives in sufficient time to arrive back at RVs. by a fixed hour. Commanders must learn to keep their eye on their watches (previously synchronised with ships' clocks) and to adhere strictly to return timings which may be either —

(i) laid down in orders, or

(ii) computed from outward timings

Frequent practice is essential to obviate delays, since the success of a raiding operation is often dependent on the length of time allowed ashore.

Re-embarkation is always a difficult problem, especially if attempted whilst in contact with the enemy. Alternative beaches should be selected whenever feasible. Experience has shown that a reserve of landing craft to replace those damaged by weather or enemy action is most desirable. They should be available off all beaches, or should patrol the extent of the coastline, keeping a sharp look-out for pre-arranged signals.

Control will repay careful study. Troops ready for re-embarkation must remain under cover NOT on, but near, the beach, and must maintain close liaison with the M.L.O., who will order them to landing craft as advised by the N.B.O.

33. Evacuation of casualties.

The problem of evacuation of casualties has never been solved satisfactorily. It is often impossible to evacuate any but walking wounded after a raid, but experiments are still being carried out with various types of collapsible stretchers.

Any wounded who are taken back to the beach must be placed in the stern of landing craft, but should NOT be embarked in first-flight craft if these have been detailed to return as second flights.

34. A.A. discipline.

One aspect of training to which we gave too little attention and which will repay a more careful study in the future is that of attuning our troops to resist the effects of dive-bombing and low M.G. attacks from the air.

With the lessons of Dunkerque still fresh in our minds, we failed lamentably to impress on our troops that the moral to the physical effect of dive-bombing is not less than 10 to 1, and that, although this form of attack both looks and sounds extremely alarming, it has little effect on the man who keeps his head.

(In Crete, where our casualties from the heaviest scale of air attack yet known were literally negligible, some of the men were badly shaken, whereas they appeared to take little notice of the German 4-inch mortar, which, in fact, produced serious casualties).

Preliminary training had been limited to practice dive attacks by single "Walrus" aircraft, which came lolloping out of the sky as unlike a "Stuka" as an owl is from a snipe. This gave exactly the wrong impression. All troops who have not previously seen action should be subjected at least once to dive attacks by a formation of modern aircraft (Hurricanes or Spitfires), whilst formidable previously concealed charges are exploded in close proximity to the trenches in which they are taking cover.

I have since tried to impress upon all ranks that A.A. drill and discipline must be perfected during training, and that the attitude towards dive-bombing which should be adopted is that of the admirable old lady who was overheard to remark to her daughter in the middle of one of the worst blitzes on London – "There's something to be said for these bombs, love – they do take your mind off the war!"

35. Later stages of training.

The later stages of Inter-Service Training should follow the lines suggested in paragraph 10 above. Schemes should include landings in bad weather and on difficult beaches. Junior Leaders must be frequently faced with the situation of finding themselves on the wrong beach, and exercises which run smoothly should sometimes be deliberately upset.

Although plans will usually include details of the whole prospective raid, both officers and N.C.Os. must realize that unforeseen circumstances may arise which render the original orders impracticable. They must therefore be prepared to act on their own initiative and to change or modify their plans, but ONLY when absolutely necessary.

Photographs and Models. Great value may be obtained from photographs and models constructed by P.R.Us. Models may be photographed obliquely from any angle, and thus give an excellent representation of the coastline and landmarks as viewed from any required direction.

Training should obviously take place on ground exactly similar to that over which the raid is to be carried out, and, if time, labour and circumstances permit, life size models of the objectives should be constructed.

36. Conclusion.

The type of man who volunteers to join a Commando normally possesses an unassuageable thirst for action, and it is sometimes difficult to maintain his interest during the long preliminary periods of training, especially if one or two prospective raids have been cancelled.

I have found that his attention to the task in hand may be stimulated by frequent repetition of the undeniable fact that every single mistake that we actually made in action need never have occurred if our previous **training** had been more **thorough**.

CHAPTER 7

COMBINED OPERATIONS PAMPHLET NO. 27
HARDENING OF COMMANDO TROOPS
FOR WARFARE

Chapters 1, 3, 4 and 5
June 1944.

Issued under the direction of the Chief of Combined Operations.

FOREWORD

The full title of this pamphlet is "Hardening of Commando troops for Warfare and notes on Field-craft." This pamphlet is a summary of lectures given by Surgeon Commander G. Murray Levick, RN, amplified as a result of experience over a number of years at special training centres in the United Kingdom.

While this pamphlet is issued mainly for the guidance of Commandos, it will also be of value to troops taking part in Combined Operations, particularly to naval parties which may have to operate for long periods ashore.

CHAPTER 1
THE HARDENING OF THE BODY
SECTION 1—GENERAL

1. There is little difference between the hardening of a greenhouse plant before putting it out into the garden and the hardening of a man to enable him to sleep in the open after living indoors. Both have mechanisms in their bodies for raising their power of resistance from a low to a high level, but these mechanisms require training before they can function efficiently.

In training men to a hard condition the following factors have to be taken into account :—

(a) Resistance to exposure.

(b) Resistance to fatigue.

SECTION 2—RESISTANCE TO EXPOSURE

2. As a result of living indoors under civilised conditions, the resistance of men to natural climates is subnormal. If a man, used to an indoor life, even if only to the extent of sleeping indoors, is transferred into a severe natural out-of-doors environment, which involves sleeping exposed to low temperatures and possibly rain, the results will be as unsatisfactory as from trying too suddenly to harden a plant. The process of hardening may in fact be delayed by calling too quickly on an undeveloped resistance.

The mechanism regulating the temperature of the body is controlled by a centre in a portion of the brain, which adjusts the balance between heat production and heat loss. The hardness of a man chiefly depends upon the training of this mechanism and this centre.

Production of heat in the body

3. The muscles are the chief source of heat in the body by their combustion of fuel food during activity, and to a lesser extent by their tone (state of constant contraction) when at rest. The heat produced by muscles is in proportion to the work they are doing.

The organs of the body also produce heat, especially during the digestion of meals. At these times the heat they produce is about equal to that produced by the muscles while the latter are at rest and producing heat only by their tone.

4. When men sleep out on a cold night, the provision of a good evening meal is important, because the body will depend largely upon the heat produced in the abdominal organs by its digestion. When awake in the early hours of the morning men feel chilly because the digestion of the evening meal has ceased, and they are getting heat from their muscle tone alone, plus a little heat produced by the heart and respiratory muscles.

When the body temperature falls, muscle tone is increased by its heat mechanism, and should this be insufficient, shivering is produced to increase heat by muscle work. In cold weather muscles are braced; in hot weather they are relaxed, to reduce heat production. This accounts for muscle flabbiness in hot climates.

Loss and retention of heat

5. The chief adjustment of heat loss is regulated thermostatically through the skin. It acts in two ways :—

(a) By a mechanism controlling the dilation and constriction of the superficial blood vessels, which thus determines the quantity of blood passing through the skin.

      (i) When this is increased, the loss of heat is increased by conduction and radiation.

      (ii) When it is decreased, the effect is reversed because the blood is kept away from the surface of the body.

(b) By special nerves to the sweat glands controlled by the heat centre.

      (i) When sweat is poured onto the skin, loss of heat is caused by evaporation, or

      (ii) When sweating stops and the skin is kept dry, loss of heat is counteracted.

6. Loss of heat by conduction through the skin is controlled by the heat centre through its action on the superficial circulation. When the body is recumbent and pressed against the ground by its own weight, much heat may be lost, especially if the ground is damp. Thus it may be better for men to lie on a ground sheet rather than use it as a covering. When lying on the ground and when clothing is dry, very little heat is lost by conduction, but as clothes become damp by sweating or rain, conduction increases, and the protection they afford decreases correspondingly.

A knowledge of these facts will assist arrangements for health and comfort under adverse conditions.

7. The loss of heat in the lungs is not automatically controlled. It occurs through evaporation on the surface of the membrane which lines the whole respiratory tract, and by conduction, by the warming of each inspiration of air which is then expired with the heat it has taken from the body. The loss of heat in this manner is perpetual and extensive.

In cold weather, when men are sleeping out, this uncontrolled loss of heat may be enough to cause subnormal body temperatures. For example, the blood temperatures in a party of six men in the Antarctic were found to range around 94 and 95 degrees Fahrenheit although under conditions less severe than often occurred.

When sleeping out on cold nights, this chilling through the lungs can be checked by lying with the head inside the sleeping bag, or by breathing through a scarf or blanket wrapped loosely round the face so that the inspired air is moistened by water vapour from expirations condensed in the wool. In this way, the evaporating power of the inspired air is reduced, and it is also warmed in its passage through the wool. This is a valuable aid in keeping warm on a cold night.

8. The term "draught" describes the chilling of a small part of the body by wind, the rest being unexposed. If most of the body is exposed, protection is effected through the sensory nerves of the skin as a whole, and a general vaso-constriction takes place. The effect of draught is chilling because the larger area of the body is not exposed to it and the sensory response to the local chilling may not be enough to cause a constriction of the skin's blood vessels. The deeper tissues of the chilled area then suffer from lack of insulation which may result in rheumatism and neuritis.

A hardened man, with his well trained heat mechanism, can resist the effects of draught better than a soft unacclimatised man. The latter may wake from a night's bivouac with a stiff neck or shoulder while the former suffers no ill effects. Nevertheless, all animals avoid draughts in choosing a bed for the night, *e.g.* a horse, seeking the shelter of a tree, never lies near the trunk, which causes a draught, but lies well away on the lee side.

The advantage of hardening is felt particularly when food supply is inadequate. In these circumstances the temperature of the body falls through lack of fuel and the retention of heat by other means becomes of supreme importance.

Men can become accustomed to a surprising degree of resistance to cold. Darwin in his "Voyage of the Beagle" states that when the "Beagle" lay off Terra del Fuego, the natives came off in canoes, naked in a freezing temperature with sleet beating on to their skins, without showing any signs of discomfort.

9. The foregoing paragraphs explain the need for gradual and sustained (not occasional) training to enable men who are unaccustomed to the rigours of warfare to gain their natural powers of resistance, so that they can keep their health under conditions which would otherwise affect them seriously. Hardening should begin at home. A dry hut is in itself a luxury compared with a bivouac in the rain. Fires in huts should therefore be abolished as a preliminary to sleeping out in the open. By hardening, men can become accustomed to a surprising degree of cold.

Officers, in particular, must ensure that the conditions of life provided in the normal officers mess do not lead to softness. Cold baths are of value. Fires in ante-rooms and a tendency to over eating combine to counteract the effect of intermittent training in the open. A tough body can only be attained through consistent habits of life.

SECTION 3—RESISTANCE TO FATIGUE

10. The training of muscles for unaccustomed stress cannot be achieved in less than a certain period of time.

When muscles are working they are bathed in a stream of fluid coming from the smaller blood vessels (capillaries) and carried away both by other capillaries and by another type of little vessels (lymphatics). This stream of fluid brings to the muscles the fuel and oxygen required for their work. The more the muscles are working, the more fuel and oxygen they need. When the oxygen supplied to a working muscle is insufficient, the muscle becomes asphyxiated. It is asphyxiation that causes the aching of muscles when they are violently exerted to their limit. The limit of such exertion is the asphyxiation point. The greater the exertion, the greater is the demand for the oxygen which can reach the muscles only through the blood stream. Therefore with unaccustomed exercise, a demand for development of extra channels is created. When the fluid stream leaves the muscles it carries away the products of muscle work (fatigue products) in the same way as a chimney carries away smoke from a fire.

The development of capillaries and lymphatics is maintained in accordance to the demand for them by the habitual work of the muscles. As this demand is increased by increased muscle work, unused channels are opened to provide for the increased need for fuel and oxygen, and for the expulsion of increased fatigue products. Habitual reduction of muscular work is followed by a proportionate obliteration of these channels.

11. The training of muscles chiefly depends upon the development of this internal circulation. This extra development of vessels takes time, and is best brought about by a *gradual* increase of muscular work. The stiffening of muscles, caused by inflammation after unaccustomed exercise is largely the result of an over accumulation of fatigue products which inflames the muscles. It may also be due to changes taking place in the working muscles through lack of fuel.

12. Whereas stiffness may be expected to a moderate extent at the outset of training, it may retard rather than increase the progress of training if carried too far. Excessive stiffening of muscles may reach a degree closely allied to actual strain and may affect one or more individual muscles and take many weeks to cure. The progressive increase of exercise in training must not exceed the rate at which the increase of vascular development in the muscles can take place. After each bout of increasing exercise a condition results, closely akin to inflammation, which causes the production of extra channels for circulation within the muscles.

This is the crux of successful training. An understanding of the above paragraphs will help officers to watch their men during training and to regulate the rate of progression.

The heart

13. A well-developed and well-exercised heart is essential to the maintenance of a good muscular circulation. If the heart is initially sound, it will gain in strength concurrently with the skeletal muscles.

Unless the heart is previously diseased, prolonged exertion cannot damage it. As the skeletal muscles become tired, the heart becomes tired too; and the more it is tired, the less it is able to strain itself. Consideration of strain, therefore, may be ignored for men with sound hearts when on the march.

A type of collapse, which is quite distinct from heart failure, seems to be inseparable from the wearing of too much tight fitting or otherwise unsuitable clothing in hot or sultry weather, especially during strenuous exertion. This interferes with the function of the skin in getting rid of heat, and men who are not in good training are especially liable to these attacks.

Attacks of this kind might be caused by the sudden exertion of running up a steep hill on a sultry day in battle dress with full equipment. Men affected collapse to the ground and, when helped to their feet, are unable to stand. This temporary paralysis of the muscles is due to complete loss of tone initiated by the heat centre in an effort to cut down heat production (see paragraph 5 above). These attacks are of short duration and only last until the men have time to cool down. Men do not lose consciousness and, after a few minutes lying down with loosened tunics, can get up and return to their duties.

A man in soft condition cannot resist exposure to cold, nor can he resist unaccustomed exposure to heat. Soldiers have to go into battle completely equipped and in heavy clothing and only well hardened men are immune to hot and sultry weather.

14. In applying these notes to training, officers must not leave themselves out of consideration, and they must find time to carry out the hard physical preparation carried out by other ranks.

SECTION 4—PROCEDURE DURING TRAINING

15. It is not possible to give more than a general guide to the procedure to be carried out while training, owing to the varying nature of the ground over which men have to be trained. The conditions of warfare for which men have to be trained are roughly as follows:—

(a) Marching and fighting over heavy sodden ground or sand deserts, involving the fatigue of muscles only lightly used in marching on roads, or on dry, level ground.

(b) Marching and fighting in hill country.

The requirements in training for sub-paragraphs (a) and (b) above are very similar. This is fortunate as it is not always possible to train troops in hill country. Men operating in hill country are to a great extent using muscles trained by traversing ploughed fields.

16. It is important to remember, however, that men trained over dry, level ground cannot stand up to the conditions in sub-paragraphs (a) and (b)

above. Therefore, if the only available country is flat, heavy ground should be chosen for training as far as possible. For instance, men should be exercised over ploughed fields, or be given spells of marching over the sands and mud flats which exist near many training areas. The fact that training for these types of conditions is identical rests on anatomical grounds.

If training on these lines is to begin when men are in the condition to be expected on leaving their training centre, the first week demands more care than any other period of the training. Mistakes in training, which result in delaying the object in view, are more frequent during the first week than at any other time. Too often the idea of giving men "a good shake up" does more to hinder than improve their state of training, and during the first few weeks the time allotted to special exercises should be short.

SECTION 5–STALENESS

17. The condition of staleness is the bugbear of coaches and of men who have to undergo prolonged periods of physical exertion. Some explanation may be found for this condition in the light of scientific research.

Causes of staleness

18. There appear to be several causes of staleness and they may or may not act concurrently. In addition to overwork, the following factors are definitely concerned:

(a) The salt factor.

(b) The nerve factor.

(c) The mental factor.

The salt factor

19. The blood, with its derivative fluid in which the tissues of the body are bathed, is normally maintained at a salinity of one per cent, and a mechanism acts to keep both this salinity and the total bulk of the blood at a constant level. When a man sweats, he sweats out water and salt. When he drinks, he replaces the water but not the salt. Repeated or prolonged sweating, therefore, gradually eliminates the salt which is needed to maintain the fluid content of the body at one per cent salinity. As this degree of salinity is essential, the body can no longer hold the water

required to keep the tissue fluids at their normal level without reducing their salinity. The body, therefore, undergoes dehydration as well as reduction of its salt.

20. Recent experiments have shown that elimination of salt from the diet produces lassitude and that this lassitude disappears when salt is restored. It is, therefore, probable that the frequent and prolonged sweating of men who are taking hard exercise for long periods, especially in hot weather or climates, will cause a scarcity of salt as well as of water, and that this is a frequent cause of staleness.

The best drink for men who are thirsty from sweating on strenuous marches is a mug of water with a dash of oatmeal (which can be carried in an empty tobacco tin) and a pinch of salt. The oatmeal makes the salt palatable. This drink both quenches the thirst and relieves it for a longer period than plain water by enabling the body to retain its normal bulk of fluids. The addition of salt to the drink must not be too great or it will produce temporary thirst. Too much salt, however, is better than too little, since the body can rid itself of excess salt through the kidneys and sweat glands.

The nerve factor

21. Exercise demands a constant output of energy from the motor nerves which drive the muscles. The more they work, the greater is the energy they must expend and the greater the nutrition they require. The centres of these nerves which are located in the spinal cord, contain a substance, visible under the microscope, which has been proved to be their reserve store of nourishment. A much fatigued animal, when killed, is found to have little or none of this substance in its nerve cells .

Two things are required for the re-stocking of these centres, the food material, and vitamin B1. The latter is essential to the conversion of the food material into the substance of the nerve cell. An ample mixed diet will provide all the food material that is needed, but the nutrition of the nerve cells must fail if the supply of vitamin B1 is inadequate. The harder the physical work the greater is the demand for Vitamin B1, so that men who are taking constant hard exercise are especially liable to that shortage of nerve energy which is a symptom of staleness.

The mental factor

22. The mechanism of the voluntary exercise of muscles is controlled by the mind. Mental effort is required all the time a man is driving his body to hard exercise. As muscles become progressively fatigued, the effort of the will to force them to act must become greater, and a time may come during long periods of training when the will power begins to fail from overwork. Concentration of the will upon movement may begin to fail during long periods of training at physical exercise just as mental concentration becomes more difficult as a result of work at intellectual subjects. In this way it may be seen how largely the mind may enter as a factor in the production of staleness in training.

Prevention of staleness

23. The prevention of staleness may therefore be summarised as follows :—

(a) *The salt factor*—Ensuring that enough salt is taken by men who are undergoing any training which involves sweating. A teaspoonful of salt should be added to each pint of water in which the oatmeal is cooked for the breakfast porridge.

(b) *The nerve centre*—Wholemeal, brown, or standard bread should be eaten in preference to white bread. Army biscuit, which is made of wholemeal, is excellent food. Oatmeal and liver are also rich in vitamin B.

(c) *The mental factor*—Monotony both in exercise and camp or barrack life should be avoided. Recreations not involving physical fatigue should be provided, and in this respect the cinema can be usefully employed in the evening. Occasional days of physical rest are desirable and, where training is the sole object in view, a day of rest should always follow any particularly strenuous day's exercise. In this way time is given for recuperation and for the progress of those developments in the body which increase endurance, and which follow after, rather than during, hard exercise.

Treatment of staleness

24. It must be realised that while men are stale nothing will be gained by exercise, which should be limited to essential duties. When men are

becoming stale a three-day holiday should be sufficient to remedy this condition, if followed by care in the future allotment of exercise.

A suggested three-day scheme is outlined below :—

(a) The salt factor should be borne in mind. This can be remedied immediately with an ordinary intake of salt when the men are resting.

(b) Concurrently with rest, particular care should be taken that an ample supply of vitamin B is included in the rations. Porridge, beans, peas, eggs and liver are foods rich in vitamin B. Meals should include plenty of green vegetables, lightly cooked or, if possible, steamed.

(c) The mental inertia resulting from staleness can be overcome by fresh interests and amusements. Mental dullness is a symptom, not a cause of staleness, but it reacts on the well-being of the body as a whole.

(d) Whereas alcohol before exercise is harmful, it may be directly beneficial for stale men if taken in moderation with the evening meal. Drunkenness, however, will certainly defeat the end in view.

CHAPTER 3
THE BIVOUAC
SECTION 11—SLEEPING AND COOKING IN THE OPEN

47. The best place for a bivouac, especially in wet weather, is inside a conifer wood, where the ground is usually porous and warm. Woods of deciduous trees are bad in wet weather as big drops of rain drop from the trees on to the fallen leaves and make the ground sodden. With this type of tree it is better to sleep outside the wood on its lee side.

48. When the ground is really wet, the most satisfactory way to make a bivouac is to make an under-mattress of branches or sticks. The latter should be one to two inches thick, the sticks being laid lengthways and just interlacing. On this spring mattress, designed to keep the body off the wet ground, is laid an upper mattress of soft vegetation such as long grass, bracken or leaves about eighteen inches in thickness. This type of bed is quite comfortable. A man can then sleep in his gas cape with his arms out of the sleeves. The soft vegetation prevents damage to the gas cape which, being waterproof, gives protection from the dampness of the vegetation.

To make a roof, unless the head is against a tree, one stake should be driven into the ground at the head end with its top a foot above the level of the head, and another into the ground at the foot of the bed, the top just clearing the feet. A piece of string tied from stake to stake will support the groundsheet cape when draped over the string. The cape is made fast to the stakes at head and foot by pieces of string.

49. Men should sleep in their boots. With a pair of dry socks, the feet will be reasonably warm even in damp boots if these are left unlaced and thrust into the pack. Any available covering should be placed over the legs from feet to knees and over the abdomen. Directions for covering the mouth are given in paragraph 7.

Cooking

50. In order to make a fire which will burn even in wet weather, two rows of holes should be bored at the bottom of a round or square tin. The holes must be close together and nearly as wide as the little finger. A fire of small dry twigs lit inside will heat water more quickly than either a Tommy Cooker or a primus stove. If the fire is made with perfectly dry twigs it is practically smokeless. Dry twigs may be found in hedges even in wet weather.

CHAPTER 4
SEASICKNESS AND IMMERSION IN WATER
SECTION 12—PREVENTION OF SEASICKNESS

51. In order to minimise the tendency to seasickness, personnel should, during training, be given every opportunity of obtaining sea experience in small landing craft in rough or choppy seas.

52. In very rough weather, or when vomiting has actually commenced, no remedy is likely to be completely effective. The following measures, however, will assist in preventing seasickness :—

(a) *General measures.*—Overcrowding on landing craft should, if possible, be avoided, and adequate ventilation ensured. The provision of as much fresh air as possible is most important. The last meal should be taken four hours before embarkation and a snack with hot tea given two hours later. When meals are taken aboard, it is preferable to eat sparingly and frequently rather than have one large meal. These measures are more important in a short than a long sea voyage, as in the shorter voyage personnel have not the same length of time to recover from seasickness or become accustomed to the movement of the ship or craft.

Personnel should be embarked in minor landing craft at the last possible moment to decrease the time spent on board. Prior to embarkation, they will normally be issued with some boiled sweets, biscuits, chewing gum and a number of vomit bags. Key personnel should be placed aft where they are not so likely to be affected.

(b) *Seasickness remedies*.—Men who are predisposed to seasickness should be given a tablet of Hyoscene Hydrobromide grain 1/100 (0.6 milligramme) one hour before embarkation and a second tablet six hours later if necessary. This tablet may cause slight dryness of the mouth, especially in hot climates.

In the case of men who are specially liable to seasickness, a tight binding, such as a puttee, round the abdomen may be of assistance.

SECTION 18—IMMERSION IN WATER AND SPRAY

53. Troops travelling in landing craft will be wet by spray and, on any except steep-to beaches, will have to wade ashore. A soldier cannot maintain his normal standard of fighting efficiency when wet, although this will be affected less in hot than in cold climates. The reasons for this loss of efficiency are as follows :—

(a) Loss of heat in the body which results in impairment of muscular action by reducing the blood supply to muscles. This not only reduces the supply of energy to the muscles, but also impairs the response of the muscles to nerve stimulus.

(b) Discomfort, amounting at times to inflammation, caused by the rubbing of wet clothes against the body, especially against the inside of the thighs and at the wrists.

(c) The additional weight of water carried in the clothes and equipment. On emerging from the water, equipment will retain water equal to 50 per cent, while clothing holds from 300 to 500 per cent of its weight.

60 per cent of this additional weight is lost in the first five minutes after emerging from the water. After that the loss in weight is slow.

54. Loss of heat through clothing becoming sodden can, to some extent, be prevented by rubbing olive oil or vaseline into the skin before embarkation.

55. Inflammation can be minimised by applying olive oil or vaseline to those parts of the body likely to be affected, by bracing the trousers as high as possible and by tucking up the shirt and vest round the waist.

56. Ground sheets should be worn across the chest to protect men and their weapons in minor landing craft from spray. The best method of preventing clothes and equipment from becoming sodden is by treating them with a water resisting solution such as Dipsanil V Cerol T or soap alum.

Drying can be accelerated by making holes 1/3in. in diameter in the battle-dress and equipment to allow water to drain out. These holes should be made as follows :—

(a) *Haversack*—Three holes in the base of the haversack; one at each end and one in the middle.

(b) *Basic pouches*—As for haversacks in sub-paragraph (a) above.

(c) *Respirator Haversack* (old style)—Three holes in the base of the respirator haversack. Two holes in each side (through the pockets); this is necessary as the respirator may be carried on the slant.

(d) *Entrenching tool case*—Five holes through both walls at the lower margin of the entrenching tool case.

(e) *Trousers*—Six holes in each trouser at the lowest part of the trouser leg when worn normally with anklets. If gas is used, the holes in the trousers will increase the vapour danger.

CHAPTER 5
THE SCIENCE OF RATIONING
SECTION 14—FOOD

57. There are three classes of organic food material. They are proteins, carbohydrates and fats.

Proteins contain carbon, oxygen, hydrogen and nitrogen. Carbohydrates and fats contain carbon, hydrogen and oxygen but no nitrogen. The tissues of the body require nitrogen, therefore only proteins can serve as building material for growth and repair of the body. Carbohydrates and fats are used purely as fuel and are burnt in the body by oxidation just as fuel is burnt in a fire, their latent energy being liberated chiefly as heat and kinetic energy.

Lean meat and white of egg are examples of almost pure protein. Starch and sugar are pure carbohydrates. Milk and eggs, the natural food of the young animal, are perfect foods containing the right proportions of building and fuel material, except that eggs contain no carbohydrates.

Nearly all vegetable foods in their natural state contain both building materials (proteins) and fuel foods (carbohydrates and fats). A mixed vegetarian diet is theoretically perfect, though a vegetarian eats less protein than a carnivorous man or animal.

58. The right proportion of the three foodstuffs in a ration is roughly as follows :—

Protein	15 per cent. of the Calories
Carbohydrates	50 " " " " "
Fat	35 " " " " "

This may be modified according to climate for reasons to be given in subsequent paragraphs.

59. Increased physical work demands an increase in the fuel foods, but not in the protein part of the ration. The carbohydrates are finally converted by digestion into a certain form of sugar (glucose) which is carried in the blood to the muscles and there burnt up to produce their heat and work energy. Fats are also broken down by digestion into fuel products which are similarly carried to the tissues by the blood. A reserve of fuel can be, and usually is, stored in the liver from the digested fuel foods in the form of glycogen. The liver discharges it into the blood stream as it is required.

60. When the full capacity of the liver is reached, further fuel food is stored about the body as fat. Proteins cannot be stored. The body gets rid of the unused protein of each meal. It is only when essential fuel foods are lacking that protein is used as fuel. This is uneconomical and unsatisfactory for health. It is better to have a mixture of carbohydrates and fat as fuel food than one of them alone, because carbohydrate helps in burning up the fat.

61. The common use of sugar in its crystalline forms and in sweet dishes and jams is unnatural for man. The cultivation of the sugar cane, and later sugar beet, leading to the consumption of large quantities of sugar, is a recent development. The natural process is for the body to make its own sugar from starch.

62. Although it is the oxidation of the fuel food which produces heat in the body, yet protein has a marked action in causing production of heat from carbohydrates and fats. This is not due to its intrinsic heat energy but to its dynamic action. This is of great importance when considering the construction of rations for a very cold climate.

During an active day the muscles produce a superabundance of heat; therefore if men are to spend cold nights in the open, the chief meal should be eaten in the evening. While on the marching ration, the pemmican or bully beef should be kept for this. The extra protein is not required so much for body building as for what has been called its specific dynamic action, referred to above.

63. The unit of energy value of foods is the Calorie. One Calorie of any foodstuff is the amount which will, when burnt, raise the temperature of a pint of water approximately 4 degrees Fahrenheit. Expressed in terms of work, it is the amount required to lift one pound 3,087 feet. In a healthy man, the net fuel value of food is approximately :—

Protein	4 Calories per gram
Carbohydrate	4 " " "
Fat	9 " " "

In making out an economical ration, it would seem at first sight best to include fat as the main fuel food owing to its high Calorie value, but in practice this is not possible because the average maximum capacity of a man for digesting fat is seven ounces a day; therefore any fuel food beyond this weight should consist exclusively of carbohydrates. Moreover, sufficient carbohydrate is needed for the optimum combustion of the fat, so it is best to mix them roughly in the proportions already stated.

64. Although most officers are not required to apply all these details directly to the making up of rations, the details will serve to explain the principles on which special rations are made up, help them in the

apportionment of the daily ration into the different meals, and guide them in the choice of alternative foods when any part of the special rations is not available.

Theoretically, the Calorie requirement of a man per diem if he weighs eleven stone is 3,365 for 24 hours if actually marching for seven hours a day, carrying no weight.

In practice, it has been found that on strenuous one-day operations, unless they are in hard training, the men are too tired to eat all they need. The demand for more fuel food, however, soon asserts itself, appetite returns, and if the men do not eat all their food at first, they should be told to save the surplus carefully for subsequent needs.

Rations in cold climates

65. Ordinary rules of dietetics hold good when applied to life in cold climates. The body reacts vigorously to the cold environment, increasing production of heat to a moderate extent by a general increase of muscular tone.

It must also be remembered that while men are marching or otherwise actively employed, the muscles, even in very cold climate, are producing an abundance of heat, and using no more fuel than they would be doing in warmer regions. This is proved by the fact that men manhauling a sledge or even just ski-ing at ordinary pace, have the inner side of their windproof outer clothing coated with frozen sweat at temperatures even of minus sixty degrees Fahrenheit. Thus, additional fuel for heat is only needed for the periods during which they are inactive.

66. In constructing a Polar ration of lightest possible weight and adequate value, it is only possible to consider the maintenance of work heat and nutrition and to disregard what has come to be known as the "sledging appetite", a torment well known to polar explorers, because it cannot be assuaged by the amount of food it is possible to carry above what is really needed. In any case, this abnormal appetite will only arise after lengthy marching, day after day, in the cold air. Nevertheless, it is important to provide enough food, for a shortage predisposes to frost bite.

Rations in hot climates

67. The food requirements for hot climates appear at first sight to be

paradoxical because natives of warm latitudes eat more fuel food and less protein, whereas those of the colder regions eat more meat in proportion to starch and sugar. The reason is the action of proteins, explained in para. 56.

In adjusting rations for hot climates, the meat portion should be reduced and, in a tropical climate, the items spread over the meals throughout the day or, in a desert climate with hot days and cool nights, concentrated into the evening meal. Cereals, green vegetables and possibly the sugar proportionately increased.

Owing to loss of salt through sweating, care should be taken to compensate this loss in the ration.

SECTION 15—VITAMINS

68. Vitamins have a direct, and important bearing on training because vitamin insufficiency in the diet may nullify the efforts made to bring the men into hard condition.

The condition resulting from a complete absence or serious deficiency of any vitamin is termed its "deficiency disease". Although the actual deficiency diseases are rare in this country, some degree of ill-health due to too small a daily supply is very common. The following are some of the essential vitamins :—

69. **Vitamin A**

(a) *Deficiency leads to*

Stunted growth.

Malnutrition.

Impaired resistance to some infections.

Dental caries.

Impaired night vision.

(b) *Common Sources of vitamin A are*

Fish livers (especially halibut).

Livers of other healthy animals.

Eggs, milk, butter, cheese (especially in spring and summer).

First grade margarine.

Carrots, tomatoes.

Green vegetables.

70. **Vitamin B1 (aneurin)**

(a) *Deficiency disease*

Beriberi. This condition is characterised by a paralysis following breakdown of the whole nervous system.

(b) *Conditions resulting from minor deficiency*

Lowering of nervous energy.

Disturbance of the pulse rate.

Premature fatigue.

Bad temper.

Neurasthenia.

Neuritis.

From the above list it will be seen that this vitamin is concerned in the nutrition of the nervous system, for which purpose it is essential.

In training for the endurance of fatigue its importance is manifest. Every movement of the muscles is brought about by the discharge of energy from the nerves which supply them, just as each ignition in a car engine is caused by the spark from the battery. The nerve centres contain a store of nutritive material which is drawn up in accordance with the energy expended by the nerves. Thus a man taking much exercise is calling upon his nerve centres for much energy and if this demand exceeds the rate at which the nutritive material can be replaced, he is "running down" his nerve centres as a car battery is run down when the discharge exceeds the charging up.

This may be a big factor in the fatigue of a long march when the supply of vitamin B1 is deficient. There is thus a lowering of stamina. It has been scientifically shown that the daily amount of vitamin B1 required by an individual varies with the exercise he takes in a proportion as great as from 200 to 500 units per diem.

The earlier onset of fatigue as well as earlier loss of wind may result from a reduced intake of oxygen in the tissues due to vitamin B1 deficiency.

Because it is not stored up in the body (as some other vitamins) the inclusion of sufficient in each meal is important for men undergoing exertion, *i.e.* in "Marching rations".

71. During recent years, nearly all civilised races have been feeding on white flour. Vitamin B1 is in the germ and skin of grains, and in the milling

of white flour it is completely removed from the wheat grain.

The standard bread of today (1944) is about 85 per cent. "whole" grain and is therefore a good source of the vitamin.

(a) *Common sources of Vitamin B1*

"Whole" cereals (brown bread, whole meal biscuits, oatmeal).

Peas and beans.

Eggs.

Milk.

Liver, sweetbreads, kidneys, brains.

(b) *Very rich sources*

Yeast.

Although moderate cooking such as the baking of bread causes only slight loss of vitamin B1, the addition of an alkali before cooking hastens the loss.

An excellent way to eat oatmeal, especially on the march, is in the form of the Scotch "brose", *i.e.* a thick paste of raw oatmeal and water with a little butter or margarine and salt. In this form it is very appetising and quickly prepared.

72. **Vitamin C**

(a) *Deficiency disease*

Scurvy.

(b) *Some conditions resulting from minor deficiency*

Lassitude and general debility.

Anaemia.

Dental caries.

Lowered resistance to disease.

Abnormal bleeding from wounds.

Delayed healing of wounds.

Rapid onset of fatigue.

Bad complexion.

(c) *Common sources of Vitamin C*

Fresh fruits, especially citrous fruits, tomatoes, rhubarb, strawberries.

Green vegetables, especially water cress, brussels sprouts, turnips, cabbage.

Pure vitamin C in the form of tablets (expensive).

All fresh vegetables and fruits contain it in varying amounts.

(d) *Important facts about Vitamin C*

It is fairly rapidly destroyed by cooking, therefore vegetables should be cooked as briefly as possible.

There is a greater concentration of the vitamin in the skins of fruits than in the flesh. In apples, the peel contains six times the concentration of vitamin found in the flesh. Stewed apples, apple tarts, dumplings, contain practically no vitamin. When soda is added to the water in which vegetables are cooked, most of the vitamin is lost.

To maintain normal health, the amount of vitamin C required is at least three times the amount required to prevent scurvy.

Lack of this vitamin would tend to spoil the efforts being made by training to get the men into hard condition.

By bio-chemical methods, the quantity of the various vitamins needed daily to maintain health under normal conditions has been ascertained. But men undergoing extra fatigue need an extra supply. The values of the various vitamins have been internationally standardised. For men living a normal life the requirements of those we have dealt with are as follows :—

Vitamin A	3000 units
Vitamin B	500 units
Vitamin C	50 milligrams

SECTION 16—CONDENSED RATIONS

73. Condensed rations are intended chiefly for men who have to carry their food supply with them. They must therefore be of the least possible weight and bulk in proportion to their value. The modern methods of dehydrating and compressing foods have revolutionised the preparation of condensed rations. Their vitamins are well preserved and the food, while in some cases reduced to an eighth of its original bulk and weight, has all the physiological properties of fresh food. To maintain health and vigour, greater accuracy is needed in the preparation of condensed rations than for those in ordinary use. Otherwise a shortage of some essential factor is likely to occur.

The principles outlined above are embodied in the War Office 24 hour ration scale, which is detailed at Appendix A [not included here]. This scale may be continued for a much longer period than the period specified without loss of health or morale. Full use has been made of the dehydrated and compressed products prepared by methods evolved at the Low Temperature Station, Cambridge, under the joint auspices of the Ministry of Food and Cambridge University. These methods ensure complete preservation of the vitamins.

74. A full list of the various condensed rations at present supplied to the Army was notified in ACIs 29 September 1943 and published by the War Office in a pamphlet entitled "Operational Feeding—Use of special Ration Packs, 1943".

CHAPTER 8

COMBINED OPERATIONS PAMPHLET NO. 24
CLIFF ASSAULTS

January 1945

SECTION 7—CLIFF CLIMBING METHODS AND DRILLS

General considerations

65. The cliff should be assaulted on as broad a front as possible. Besides the reasons detailed in paragraph 53 above [not included here], the fact that there will be handlines available over a wide front will help the speed and efficiency with which follow-up troops can clear the beaches. In the case of a rocky landing, handlines will be led up from a series of distinct points, and craft containing follow-up troops must be directed to such points only.

66. On a variable cliff, some parts of which appear to be surmountable by climbing methods while other parts necessitate mechanical aids, the ropes placed by the rocket throwers may not always be in the most convenient positions. Where, however, the cliff has been climbed without aids, the handlines running down will be at easy angles, and trained troops using them will clear the beach rapidly.

67. If the time of landing is at night, and there is a possibility of achieving surprise, pure climbing methods are quiet, and can be performed quickly by the drill outlined in paragraphs 69–91.

68. Climbing requires a higher degree of individual and sub-unit training than does scaling with mechanical aids. The latter does mechanically much of that which in climbing has to be done by the individual. The following climbing methods and drills, modified as required, will consistently also be found suitable for scaling.

Assault wave organization

69. The troops should be organized as follows :—

    (a) Climbing leaders who will be sufficient in number to ensure that the selected cliff is covered on a wide enough front.

    (b) Climbing "seconds," who also take up ropes once the leaders are up.

    (c) A party to provide early covering fire to protect the actual rope heads.

    (d) The main body of assault troops to form the main bridgehead.

    (e) Signal personnel to establish communications on the beach.

    (f) Signal personnel to establish communications from the main bridgehead.

    (g) Liaison men from follow-up troops. These will be equipped with rollers, etc. if the follow-up troops include heavily laden personnel who will require assistance in getting up the cliff.

Assault wave climbing equipment

70. **Climbing leaders**—Climbing leaders will land with a gripfast strapped round their waists. A 1½ inch alpine rope will already have been secured to the gripfast, the rest of the rope being handcoiled in baskets on their backs. They will wear climbing boots. If the cliff is not hard rock, they will carry cut-down ice axes. If there is a lip, or a short patch of vertical earth or gravel at the cliff top, they will also carry hand grapnels or hand grapnel carriers which will help them over this. They will be armed with pistols.

71. **Climbing "seconds"**—Climbing "seconds" will land with a gripfast strapped round their waist and a 2½ inch rope coiled in baskets and secured to the gripfast ring. They will wear climbing boots and carry pistols and machine carbines.

72. **Party providing covering fire**—The party providing covering fire will wear climbing boots for speed, and will carry machine carbines and hand grenades.

73. **Main body**—The main body will carry normal infantry platoon weapons and equipment unless particular obstacles are expected inland. Climbing boots will usually be worn.

74. **Signals on the bridgehead**—Signal equipment required on the bridgehead will be :—

    (a) Wireless sets SCR 536.

    (b) Light telephone Mark M, or sound power telephone. Twisted cable on light rollers and W 130. This will provide a telephone link between the bridgehead and the beach.

75. **Signals on the beach**—Signal equipment required on the beach will be :—

    (a) Wireless sets No. 38 or No. 68.

    (b) Beach markings, with lights for use at night.

    (c) Morse torches.

76. **Liaison men**—Liaison men will carry rollers, gripfasts and coiled ropes to assist follow-up troops in climbing the cliff.

Day or night assault drill

77. **Landing drill**—

    (a) On touching down, the leaders will land first, followed by the "seconds" and the party providing covering fire. These parties will be split up among the first wave of landing craft.

    (b) The main body will fan out at the cliff foot following the leader's general direction from each landing craft.

    (c) A party from the main body will guard the beach flanks and will also take up a position from which they can keep the cliff head under observation in order to protect the leaders while climbing.

78. **Climbing drill**—

    (a) The leaders will discard their baskets containing the coiled 1½ inch rope at the cliff foot, and with the end of the rope already fastened to their gripfasts, will climb the cliff by the quickest routes they can find.

    (b) The "seconds" will pay out the leaders' ropes from the basket. 1½ inch rope is used as heavier rope would impede climbing.

    (c) The leaders on reaching the top will crawl over, unhitch their gripfasts and will push the prongs in the ground. They will then give two heaves on the rope as a signal.

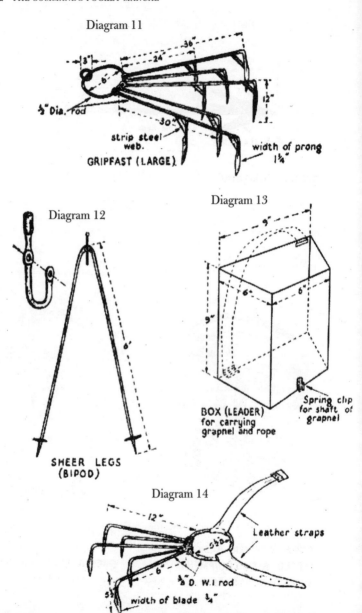

Diagram 11

½" Dia. rod

strip steel web.

GRIPFAST (LARGE)

width of prong 1¼"

Diagram 12

Diagram 13

SHEER LEGS (BIPOD)

BOX (LEADER) for carrying grapnel and rope

Spring clip for shaft of grapnel

Diagram 14

Leather straps

⅝" D. W.I rod

width of blade ¾"

Diagram 15

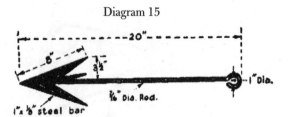

LIGHT THROWING GRAPNEL WITH FIVE PRONGS

Diagram 16

Diagram 17

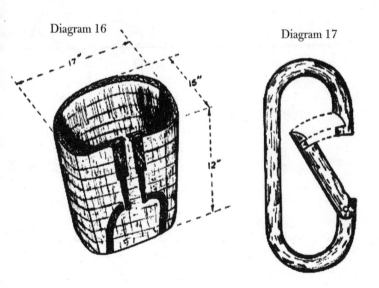

ROPE CARRIER BASKET
FITTED WITH EQUIPMENT
SHOULDER STRAPS

SPRING LINK (KARABINER)

(d) The "seconds," on receiving the signal, will climb the cliff, using the leaders' ropes as landlines. Their rope will also be run up as they climb, being paid out from the basket by a man at the bottom. On reaching the cliff top, or any point where the angle becomes easy, they will give two heaves on the rope as a signal for the leading members of the covering fire party to ascend the leaders' ropes.

(e) Each "second" will then crawl to his leader, unhitch his gripfast (which will then be fastened in the ground by the leader) and will move forward to give the leader cover with his machine carbine.

(f) The leader, when the "second's" gripfast is in, will give two heaves on the "second's" rope, which will then be ready for use. This rope being thicker will be easier to climb. The leader will look after both ropes.

(g) After the initial men of the covering party are on the cliff top, they will be followed by the bridgehead commander, the signal party with the telephone and the main assault party to form the bridgehead in accordance with the plan.

(h) The personnel carrying rollers, etc. will place them in suitable positions, reporting these positions to the beachmaster.

(j) If the cliff is steep, only one man will be able to use a handline at one time. When he has finished using it, he will give two heaves on it as a signal to the next man, who will be holding the lower end, to ascend the cliff, his place at the bottom of the handline being taken by another man.

(k) The order of climbing for the various parts of the main body with each set of ropes must be worked out beforehand.

(l) Certain rope positions always prove much easier for ascent than others. It is the beachmaster's responsibility to ensure that bodies of men are directed to the easier places as soon as they disembark from the landing craft.

Formation of assault bridgehead at night

79. (a) A drill for the formation of a bridgehead at night is necessary to ensure a steady flow of men up the cliff.

(b) The bridgehead commander will select a control point in the centre of the bridgehead and if possible under cover. White tapes will be run to the control point from the outermost gripfasts on either flank. The main body proceeding up any rope will follow the tapes and pass through the control point.

(c) White tapes will be run out from the control points to :—

(i) The right and left flanks, where sub-units will be forming the bridgehead perimeter.

(ii) The bridgehead headquarters. This must not be too close to the edge of the cliff.

(d) The main body will pass though the control point, follow the appropriate tapes, and form up in its correct position on the outer perimeter, not too close to the cliff head.

(e) The parties on the left and right flanks will report when they are in position, and the bridgehead commander will call in the initial covering fire party by signal. This party will move up to bridgehead headquarters to form a small reserve with high fire power. They will usually take up a position just forward of this headquarters, as the final link-up of the two flanks may take a long time in the dark.

(f) The use of a password and countersign is essential.

Follow-up wave—link up with the initial assault

80. The bridgehead commander, when he considers the situation suitable, will call in the follow-up troops by R/T, using codewords.

81. At night, it is often difficult to direct men quickly to the rope positions, particularly if there is a wide beach to be crossed. A transverse white tape should, therefore, be laid by the beachmaster between port and starboard lights, and white tapes run out from each pair of ropes in use to the transverse tape. The men will then be guided to the end of the ropes and will avoid going into gullies, etc. up which no ropes have been led. This procedure is necessary, particularly for deeply indented cliffs.

Climbing personnel within the follow-up troops

82. There should be some climbers with rope baskets and gripfasts amongst the follow-up troops in case :—

(a) The initial assault has heavy casualties and there are not enough ropes in position.

(b) The initial assault lands on the wrong beach and the cliff assault force commander, coming in later with the follow-up troops, decides to assault the correct beach.

83. If the initial assault is successful, and the ropes are in position, climbers of the follow-up troops will ascend the cliff carrying their ropes and gripfasts, and dump them with the leaders at the top. The latter can then put in the gripfasts and throw the ropes down. These extra ropes will enable the beach to be cleared quicker, and will provide more means for withdrawal in cases where the cliff assault is a raiding operation only, terminated by re-embarkation.

Reorganization of the follow-up troops at the cliff top

84. Parties going up the handlines are liable to get split up and mixed, and must re-form into their sub-units before the force can move out of the bridgehead. In daylight sub-unit commanders will lead their sub-units to particular ropes and the sub-units will reform at the top. At night, particularly if the landing is opposed on the beaches, such organization may be impossible. Personnel of one sub-unit may go up different rope groups and sometimes individuals or sub-units will be shifted by the beachmaster to easier places.

The following procedure, therefore, will be adopted to reform mixed bodies as quickly as possible into sub-units. In addition to the white tapes already laid by the initial assault party from the outer flank gripfast to the control point, more white tapes will be laid from the control point to areas within the bridgehead which have been allotted to each of the main units taking part. In the case of a commando with, for instance, A and B troops used as the initial wave, tapes would be run out for C, D and E troops, the heavy weapons troop and headquarters troop. A liaison officer or NCO will be posted at the control point to ensure that personnel follow along the correct tape. Phosphorescent signs will make the routes more easily visible. In this way, whatever ropes are used, all personnel will pass through the control point and thence to their correct forming up area. Medical personnel will remain near the control point and will carry out cliff evacuation from there.

A diagrammatic layout of the bridgehead, showing the guiding tapes diverging from the control point, is shown at Appendix D.

Heavily laden personnel

85. Personnel of the medium machine gun or 3 inch mortar sections may have difficulty in getting up steep handlines. Such men can be helped up by a hauling team at the cliff top, equipped with rollers and a looped rope. The hauling team with their equipment should be landed with the assault wave. They should choose a suitable area and get their apparatus erected as soon as possible. The beachmaster must be informed of the position of this area and in daylight it should be indicated by a sign on the beach. At night, all heavily laden personnel should report to the beach centre light where a guide will direct them to the places where the rollers have been erected.

Heavy stores

86. Heavy stores in addition to the equipment referred to in paragraph 85 above, will probably have to be hauled up the cliff. Trained haulage teams will be required for this task. They will be equipped with a bipod, from which a stay (usually the end of the hauling rope) is attached to a gripfast. A second rope, attached to gripfasts at the cliff top, will be stretched taut and passed through a spring link clipped on the bipod, and made fast to a boulder or sand hook at the bottom of the cliff. Stores are tied on the haulage rope with simple non-jamming hitches, and suspended from the stretched rope with light snatch pulleys or spring links. A simple system of heaves on the hauling line serves for signalling. Stores can be raised at greater speed by use of a haulage bag, consisting of a large canvas bag on a metal rod with fittings for suspending it to the stretched rope. When the load reaches the top of the cliff, the bipod is swung back. The load lands on the cliff top, where it is undone (or taken out of the bag), and removed to a dump in a central position within the bridgehead.

Casualty evacuation

87. There are two main problems in casualty evacuation —

    (a) Getting casualties down a cliff to be evacuated by sea.

    (b) Getting casualties up a cliff to a regimental aid post forward.

88. The casualty to be lowered down a cliff is strapped in a naval "Neil Robertson" stretcher, which is suspended from the stretched rope of a haulage apparatus by spring links at either end of the stretcher. The stretcher is then lowered away from above. Besides the loops at either end of the stretcher a central suspension is needed. This is obtained by threading a line through the four carrying handles, bringing together the four loops so formed, and clipping them in a spring link. This spring link is clipped to the stretched rope with another spring link. Nine-inch diameter rope loops should be attached to either end of the stretcher to facilitate clipping on.

89. Where cliff surfaces are irregular or their gradients not steep enough to allow of good "air clearance" for the stretched rope as described in paragraph 88, an alternative method is as follows.

A haulage team is used and a stretcher bearer escorts the "Neil Robertson" stretcher. A line loop is passed through the stretcher's lower pair of rope handles and across the escort's back and over one shoulder.

The stretcher is supported in this way at hip level and allows complete freedom of manoeuvre for the escort who holds his stretcher with one hand at either end, leans well back at right angles to the cliff face and so can choose his route up or down.

Almost the whole weight of the stretcher is taken by the haulage rope. This rope is tied to the stretcher head leaving 12 feet of slack end; the escort ties himself on to this free end with a bowline round his waist.

In a cliff ascent, when the stretcher head reaches the cliff top the haulage pull at once becomes horizontal instead of vertical. At this point the escort detaches the line loop from across his shoulder and, still belayed through the head of the stretcher to the haulage rope, takes his stand immediately below the cliff top and assists the haulage team in passing the stretcher over the cliff edge.

A roller is used for ascents, but not for descents.

90. When a casualty is being raised up a cliff, the stretcher is suspended on the stretched rope as above, and the hauling rope is taken over a roller between the bipod legs. The roller eases the friction, and the casualty is hauled up and landed at the top in the usual way.

Using a roller at the cliff edge, the bearer and stretcher are hauled up, the bearer again leaning outwards from the cliff. If the extreme top portion of the cliff is vertical, this method demands considerable strength on the part of the bearer.

Cliff withdrawals

91. Cliff withdrawals are difficult to do smoothly. A carefully prepared timetable will have to be made, and considerable individual training will have to be done in the technique of roping down a cliff, particularly in the dark.

92. The withdrawal should take place in three main stages :—

(a) Returning troops will form up inside the bridgehead, and sub-unit commanders will report to the bridgehead commander when they are ready. The bridgehead commander will give the order for the withdrawal by sub-units, and will give orders for the appropriate craft to be called in. If it is dark, beach lights must be turned on.

(b) All outlying troops having been withdrawn, a close-support party on an inner perimeter will be put out covering the rope heads. The main body of the bridgehead will then withdraw on orders from the bridgehead commander. The bridgehead commander will withdraw his headquarters to the control point, and each sub-unit will report to the control point as it passes through.

(c) Finally a "crash" withdrawal will be carried out by the close-support party and the leaders. These men should be selected for their speed in roping down.

In the dark, such withdrawals will be greatly facilitated if subsidiary white tapes are run to the heads of the ropes from the two main tapes which lead from the outmost gripfasts to the control point. (*See* diagram at Appendix D). Also confusion will be avoided if such ropes are previously grouped in groups of four.

If there is a sandy beach, such withdrawals can be speeded up by erecting several bipods at the top, with a stretched rope leading down from them to a sand hook securely buried at the bottom. All men will carry a toggle rope, or a rope loop with a spring link, and either pass it over the stretched rope, or clip on and go down on a "death slide". Men trained in this method of roping down will be able to carry out a very fast withdrawal.

APPENDIX D
DIAGRAMMATIC LAYOUT OF A CLIFF BRIDGEHEAD
SHOWING THE POSITION OF GUIDING TAPES

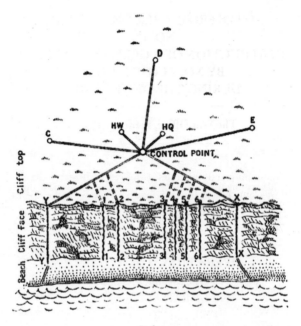

Reference

C, D, E	=	C, D and E Troop forming up positions.
HW	=	Heavy Weapon Troop forming up position.
HQ	=	Headquarter Troop forming up position.
▬▬▬	=	Main guiding tapes both on beach and cliff top.
◄▬▬►	=	Subsidery guiding tapes, for use in withdrawal.
Y, X	=	Outermost ropes on each flank.
1, 2, 3, 4, 5, 6	=	Climbing ropes, preferably grouped in pairs of fours.

CHAPTER 9

NOTES FROM THEATRES OF WAR
NO. 11
DESTRUCTION OF A GERMAN BATTERY
BY NO. 4 COMMANDO
DURING THE DIEPPE RAID

The War Office, February 1943.

No. 1 Communique. 0600 hours, 19th August, 1942.
"A raid was launched in the early hours of to-day on the DIEPPE area of enemy-occupied FRANCE."
BBC 0700 hours.

OPERATION "CAULDRON"
A classic example of the use of :—
WELL TRAINED INFANTRY.
FIRE and MOVEMENT.
The killing power of INFANTRY WEAPONS in the attack.
THOROUGHNESS IN TRAINING, PLANNING,
and EXECUTION.

VARENGEVILLE
19TH AUGUST, 1942

At daybreak No. 4 Commando, consisting of 252 all ranks including seven Allied personnel, assaulted the 6-gun battery at Varengeville. The position was defended by an approximately equal number of Germans, with all the advantages of concrete, wire and mines, concealed MGs, mortars, dual purpose flak guns, and knowledge of the ground. They had had two years to perfect these defences and when the time came they fought with the greatest determination. Yet, within 100 minutes of the landings, the position was overrun. The battery and all its works were totally destroyed, and at least 150 Germans left dead on the ground. Prisoners were also taken. British casualties were 45, of whom 12 were back at duty within two months.

INTRODUCTION

1. *General*

Operation "CAULDRON" is an outstanding example of what can be achieved by troops armed only with infantry weapons and by gallantry, sound planning, and thorough training.

It is a model of "fire and movement" tactics. Frontal fire pinned the enemy to the ground while the assault troops moved round their flank to the forming up position, the assault itself being preceded by a final crescendo of fire. The principle of this attack and that of the battle drill taught at the School of Infantry are the same.

This account is published in order that all may benefit from the story of a stimulating achievement. To obtain full value from it, officers and NCOs should first study it as an indoor exercise and then be told what happened on the day.

It should be borne in mind that this is merely an episode in a major operation in which the main brunt of the fighting was borne by the Canadian forces.

2. *Planning*

The soundness of the plan is a major factor in any success. This observation is true of operation "CAULDRON." The plan was simple, flexible, and understood by all ranks. Its thoroughness was based on a detailed study of the information obtained from German dispositions. It was animated by the will to gain surprise.

However, good plans are not enough to command success; they must be completed by skilful and determined execution.

3. *Training*

Waterloo may or may not have been won on the playing fields of Eton; it is certainly much truer to say that operation "CAULDRON" was won on the training fields of England. The remarkable features of the training were the : –

(a) Accuracy with which the nature of the various actions was foreseen.

(b) Soundness of the training programme, which resulted in the soldier's meeting the sudden events of the day with the confidence of a highly trained athlete hearing the expected starting pistol for his race.

(c) Implicit confidence of the troops in their weapons, the culmination of months of practice in all phases of the FIRE FIGHT.

All operations have special features for which special training is needed. In this one, cliff climbing, the use of scaling ladders, employment of Bangalore torpedoes under unusual conditions, and measures for embarkation and re-embarkation needed special treatment. This was given until, as in all else, perfection was reached.

A point which most people would miss was the elaborate care with which the seating arrangements in the landing craft had to be made. A reorganization on the beaches would have meant death to many. It was not until after a heart·breaking number of trials that the right solution was arrived at.

Details of training are shown at Appendix A [not included here].

4. *Execution of the plan*

It should be borne in mind that this Commando attack was a purely infantry operation, unassisted by other arms.

The operation brings out, yet again, how much the inflicting of heavy enemy casualties at comparatively light cost to ourselves is due to a sound appreciation of infantry fire power and to the team work, efficiency, and discipline of the troops.

It is interesting to note the high number of Germans killed by infantry weapons whilst behind cover. This success was due to the special training of the troops in "accuracy shooting."

The application of successful mortar fire throughout the operation—the 3-inch from an OP 800 yards in front of the base plate, using both line and RT, the 2-inch boldly used in its correct role—is a lesson to all.

The high number of casualties scored by rifles and Bren guns fired from the hip at short range during the actual assault was a just reward of the previous careful training.

5. *Lessons*

Lessons, that should be looked for in the account of the action, are :—

(a) *Weapons*

Rifle.—The large number of Germans who fell to our rifles had had their death sentences signed many months before when the commando struggled to perfection in judging distance and shooting straight.

Sniper.—A special mention must be made of the snipers. It was made very clear to the Germans that a stalker with a quick and sure eye, cunning, and field craft, and the sniper's rifle with its telescopic sight, can do much to swing the battle against them.

Bayonet.—There is something about a bayonet that defeats not only the armchair critic but, what is more important, the enemy. The Hun has always hated it. He may be old-fashioned but it can't be helped.

EY Rifle and grenades.—The EY rifle and 68 grenade were useful against enemy behind defences but the incendiary bullet was not a success. Its use invariably drew fire. 36 grenades were useful, though it appears that the Germans can throw their stick grenades farther.

Bren gun.—The Bren gun did what was expected of it. Thanks to concentration on judging of distance, accuracy of fire, and the use of cover, many Germans were killed by Bren fire. Considerable training in firing it from the hip during the assault produced striking results.

Tracer.—It was agreed that the psychological effect of tracer at night is very great. It is necessary that this form of battle inoculation should be undertaken without delay. The demoralizing effect of tracer, which always appears to be going to hit you, is very great.

Mortars, 2-inch and 3-inch.—Extensive training and practice was undertaken to ensure a high degree of accuracy and speed in obtaining fire effect.

During the operation, as the narrative shows, this training probably went far to ensure the successful end of the operation.

TMC.—Extensive training in the use of the TMC in assault and in-fighting was undertaken. Results obtained were good, but the Bren proved a more effective weapon when used from the hip in similar circumstances.

(b) *Minor tactics*

Training in fire and movement was carried out over country similar to that fought over, with special regard to close country fighting. All ranks were thoroughly prepared for their various parts in all phases of the action. This careful study and preparation was the main reason why such a small infantry force was able to defeat approximately equal numbers of an enemy who was organized behind wire and occupying strong prepared defences.

Training in the use of smoke at the right time and place, and in suitable quantity, resulted in the saving of many casualties at critical moments.

The success obtained in this operation bears out the principle of thorough and detailed training in the basic infantry requirements—FIRE and MOVEMENT.

PART I.—THE PROBLEM

1. Object

"CAULDRON" Force's orders were to destroy the battery near VARENGEVILLE with all speed and at all cost. This preliminary operation was essential to the larger plan, since the battery covered the Dieppe approaches and it was not possible to send in the large landing craft until it had been silenced. "CAULDRON" Force landings were not to begin before 0450 hours.

2. Ground

The attached sketch map [overleaf] shows all features of significance that could be detected from air photographs.

The battery position near VARENGEVILLE (three and a half miles WEST of DIEPPE) is 1100 yards from the sea front. The cliffs are steep except at Beach One and Beach Two. At Beach One two precipitous gulleys led up to wooded country running within 300 yards of the battery. Beach Two, near the mouth of the river Saane, appeared the next possible landing place.

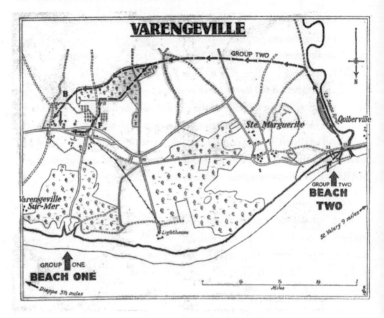

A photograph of the chimney on Beach One is shown in the appendices [not included here].

3. Defences

Air photographs showed no indication of defences along the cliffs or at Beach One.

(a) *Beach One*

In the battery area, wire could be seen on all sides except to the west. The gun positions (2) were seen to be contiguous. Two light AA guns were located at (3) and (4). Only one MG position (5) was definitely located, but it was expected that others were similarly placed to cover the re-entrant angles of the wire and the road approaches. An overhead cable (6) led from the battery position to the lighthouse. This was thought to be an OP. Last-minute reconnaissance reported two light AA guns in the lighthouse area. This battery area was considerably built over and consequently difficult to interpret. Subsequent events, however, revealed that the intelligence, in general, was correct. Additional information is shown on the sketch map and will be described during the narrative.

(b) *Beach Two*

At Beach Two traces of wire were seen on the beaches and at (22), at the western extremity of the cliff line, were two pillboxes covering the beaches and the flat ground at the mouth of the River Saane.

Inland of Beach Two, a complicated network of trenches, wire, and MG posts could be seen on the high ground to the right of the village of ST. MARGUERITE covering the valley of the River Saane.

4. The enemy

From intelligence reports it was known that the battery and its protective troops belonged to the 110 Division, a first-class formation which had seen hard fighting in Russia. Reports also suggested an infantry company located in the ST. MARGUERITE battery area and another in the QUIBERVILLE area.

PART II.– THE PLAN

1. The plan of OC "CAULDRON" Force was to hold the enemy with covering fire from the coast side of the battery while the assault was launched from inland.

2. He divided his command into two groups for this purpose. Group 1 was to provide the covering fire and Group 2 was to carry out the assault.

3. GROUP 1, a total of 88 all ranks, consisted of:—

Group HQ.	Signal Section
"C" Troop, 4 Commando*	IO, MO, RSM
Fighting patrol "A" Troop,	R Naval Beach Master
4. Commando	Allied personnel
Signal mortar detachment.	Reserve ammunition carrying party

It was to land at first light on Beach One and :—

(a) form a bridgehead above the cliff, both for the advance and to cover the withdrawal.

*Troop HQ+two sections = three officers, 52 ORs.

(b) engage the battery frontally with small arms fire as soon as the alarm was raised or the battery itself had opened fire on the main landing at Dieppe. They were not to close with the battery until Group 2 had captured the battery position.

A reinforcement of ten men carrying additional 3-in. mortar ammunition was to be landed after daylight. This party was also to lay and light No. 18 smoke generators on the beach to cover the withdrawal.

4. GROUP 2, a total of 164 all ranks, consisting of :—

CO "CAULDRON" Force

Force Headquarters

"A" Troop (less one fighting patrol), 4 Commando

"B" Troop, 4 Commando

"F" Troop, 4 Commando

Allied personnel was to land on Beach Two in two waves

5. "A" Troop, less one section, was to land on Beach Two to the left of the River Saane. Its tasks were :—

(a) to cover from the WEST the assault on the battery position.

(b) during the withdrawal to protect the flank from attack from the WEST.

The first wave, in one LCA*, consisting of a section of "A" Troop, was to land, under cover of fire from a LCS† at the left end of Beach Two and overcome any immediate opposition to the landing of the second wave, particularly from the two pillboxes. It was then to move by the shortest route to the area double crossroads (10) to prevent the enemy in ST. MARGUERITE from interfering with the assault on the battery.

The remainder of Group 2, in four LCAs, were to land on Beach Two.

The second wave, consisting of "B" and "F" Troops and Force HQ, was to follow after a three-minute interval, slightly farther to the right on the

---

* LCA (Landing craft, assault). A flat bottomed boat approximately 35 feet long by 9 feet wide, drawing about 3 feet at the stern. Carries maximum 35 soldiers. Crew of one naval officer and three ratings. Square bows, lowered to form ramp for disembarkation.

† LCS (Landing craft, support). A flat bottomed boat same size as LCA, not meant to carry troops. No disembarkation ramps. Armed with Orlikon and/or 3-inch mortar for smoke and twin, dual purpose Lewis guns.

beach. This force was then to move at all possible speed up the valley of the Saane for about 1,000 yards, and then turn left and move a further 1,900 yards to a wood (19). The LCS was to lie off Beach Two and oppose by fire any attempt to bring up reinforcements from the Quiberville area along the coast road.

Alternative plans were prepared for use if the landing was delayed. Their object was to shorten the approach to the objective should the landing take place in daylight. If there was slight delay the main force was to take the same direct route as the section of "A" Troop. If the delay was considerable, the landing of the entire force on Beach One was envisaged.

The assault was to be delivered by "B" and "F" Troops from the wooded area inland from the battery position. 90 minutes were allowed for the approach from the beach to the forming up position. Covering fire was to be provided by "C" Troop from the front of the position and "A" Troop. A squadron of four-cannon Hurricanes were to 'shoot up' the battery position at Z+90. The signal for the assault was three white Verey lights supplemented by RT messages.

6. *Points in planning worth noting*

(a) During the approach to the beach, the landing craft were to provide covering fire for the initial landing if required. This responsibility was jointly that of the military personnel with their automatic weapons and of the naval crews with stripped Lewis guns.*

(b) All papers and means of identification, other than identity discs, were to be removed from personnel.

(c) *Weapons and equipment*

(i.) All troops except "C" Troop, carried their normal weapons. "C" Troop carried two extra LMGs and an anti-tank rifle, together with four discharger cups and four snipers' rifles with telescopic sights.

(ii.) Grenades were to be primed, magazines filled, and all arms and equipment checked in daylight the day before the operation.

---

*Naval crews have their primary task in working the craft and, therefore, covering fire should normally be provided by the military personal in the craft.

(iii.) Ammunition and explosives to be taken were considerable, and therefore had to be widely distributed; no rations or water bottles could be carried. 1,000 rounds ·45 and 1,000 rounds ·303 reserve were to be landed on Beach One, and, in addition, 3,000 rounds reserve ·303 remained in LCAs. No. 36 grenades were carried by all riflemen, and a useful number of No. 77 (phosphorus) grenades were taken. Incendiary bombs and bullets were also carried.

Made up charges were to be carried for destroying the guns and installations.

(d) *Intercommunication*

RT communication was to be established between both Group HQs and to all Troops. Intercommunication between Group 1, "C" Troop, Beach Signal Station, and LCA was by No. 18 Sets; between Group 1, Group 2, and within Group 2, by No. 38 Sets. (These communications worked excellently. In addition, various links manned by attached personnel were established from Beach One to the beach used by the Canadians on the left flank, with Force HQ and with the naval landing craft).

PART III.— THE NARRATIVE

1. Group 1

At 0430 hours Group 1 were approaching Beach One. The lighthouse was flashing, but a few minutes afterwards it suddenly cut off and a few seconds later some white star shells went up from the semaphore tower beside the lighthouse. The LCA commander was asked to increase speed if possible, since surprise had apparently been lost. It was not easy to see the beach; the flare from the lighthouse had served as a useful navigational guide, and greater precision was obtained by recognition of two white houses on the cliff which had been memorized from air photographs.

The two LCAs went in according to plan, and, by the sound seamanship of the Navy, arrived within a yard of the correct place. Troops disembarked in successive waves and because of the prearranged plan for seating in the LCAs no reorganization was necessary on landing. Troops stepped ashore on to dry land. Previous experience had shown that automatic weapons and particularly TMCs are likely to jam after a wetting. As it was, one Bren gun, which had been kept pointing over the bows of one of the LCAs, had been splashed by a wave and was very sluggish until the lubrication warmed up.

It was high tide, and in less than a minute the whole of Group 1 was under the cliffs. The leading sub-section of "C" Troop started up the left-hand cleft, but returned very soon to report that it was impassable. It was partly filled up by falls of cliff and was also very heavily wired. The right hand chimney was then tried, and two Bangalore torpedoes were blown in the wire which also choked this exit. The cliffs were unscaleable and time was of paramount importance. It was realized that the use of explosives was likely to sacrifice surprise, but progress otherwise was impossible.

Fortunately the explosions coincided with heavy firing farther down the coast and were not apparently heard at the battery position. The Group pushed on as fast as possible with their first task. 1 Section, "C" Troop, went forward to the front edge of the wood facing the battery, after searching some houses on the way. From 2 Section, one sub-section searched all the remaining houses and ground in the immediate vicinity of Beach One, while the second sub-section guarded the bridgehead around the gulley.

"A" Troop's fighting patrol, after cutting the telephone cable from the lighthouse OP, worked round to the right of the battery and, after "C" Troop went into action, engaged the gun sites from windows of adjoining houses with accurate small arms fire at a range of about 250 yards. This patrol also silenced the west flak gun, killing three successive gun crews. 1 Section of "C" Troop entered a small salient strip of scrub (12) facing the forward wire of the battery 250 yards in front of them. Some of the enemy, including what appeared to be a cook in a white suit, were standing about unconcernedly, thus suggesting that complete surprise had been achieved.

The mortar OP was established, and the linesman went back uncoiling the wire; the time was now 0530 hours. Owing to an error of judgment on the part of the corporal-IC mortar, who moved his mortar further forward than necessary, time was lost, and it was able to open fire only just before the final assault. Line communication failed and communication from the OP was from the Group Commander's No. 18 set to "C" Troop set, an arrangement which had already been anticipated and practised.

By 0540 hours No. 2 Section of "C" Troop were in position between (12) and (13) and the battery was being heavily engaged by small arms fire. The three Bren guns fired in short bursts on a prearranged plan, only one gun firing at a time; it was necessary to weigh the conflicting claims of making the maximum display possible from this direction and at the same time conserving ammunition. Each gun had 16 magazines of which about 12 were fired. One was continually in action in a position in long grass only 150 yards from the battery and was not observed. Three men with snipers' rifles did excellent work. One of them, his face and hands painted green, and wearing suitable camouflage, crawled forward to a fire position 120 yards from the gun emplacement.

These snipers had been issued with incendiary bullets as well as SAA to fire at the wooden battery buildings. This arrangement was probably a mistake, since the chances of setting a house on fire with an incendiary bullet are small, and their use seldom failed to draw fire. All three enemy MG positions at (7), (5), and (8) were successively silenced by the accurate shooting of these Bren gunners and snipers. The anti-tank rifle was used against all buildings from which fire appeared to be coming, but it was hard to judge its effectiveness; 60 rounds were fired by the gunner, mostly rapid, at the flak tower in rear of the gun sites. Two EY rifles were also taken. The gun emplacements were out of range, but a 68 grenade was fired through the window of a house to silence a sniper. A short time after the enemy had been engaged with small arms fire, the 2-inch mortar arrived. The first bomb fell short, but the second hit one of the cordite dumps behind the guns and a blinding flash resulted. The time was now 0607 hours and the battery never fired again. All efforts at fire fighting were prevented by accurate small arms fire.

The fire travelled and other cordite dumps exploded, severely burning the German gun crews. The 2-inch mortar continued to give accurate fire behind the gun emplacements. Small arms fire and mortar fire (with smoke just before zero hour for the assault) continued until the assault signal went up at about 0630 hours. A few minutes later a German 80-mm. mortar, firing from east of the battery position, got the range just as the party was beginning to withdraw, and the first three casualties occurred. Hitherto, enemy fire (mortar, heavy MG, and horizontal flak) had been consistent but inaccurate, being mostly too high. It is thought that the 2-inch mortar position was given away when it started to fire smoke by the trails that these bombs leave while passing through the air.

Meanwhile, the remainder of "C" Troop had searched all the houses above the beach and the surrounding cover, killing enemy snipers. The overhead cable from the lighthouse OP to the battery had been destroyed. The five or six salvos fired by the battery at the shipping off Dieppe all fell short; their failure was probably due to the cutting of this line.

Attention must now be turned from this success to the flank attack of Group 2.

2. Group 2

The five LCAs and one LCS containing Group 2 also increased speed when the white star shells went up from the lighthouse at 0430 hours. As "A" Troop (less one section) disembarked and began to cross the heavy beach wire (14) they came under mortar and MG fire and had four casualties. The remainder of the Group at once began to go ashore 150 yards farther up the beach, using rabbit netting to get across the wire. They also came under fire and received eight casualties. The enemy used a concentration of tracer ammunition which, in the half light, had a most unpleasant effect on men not accustomed to it. There seems to be some doubt whether this fire was coming from high ground west of ST. MARGUERITE or from the QUIBERVILLE direction, or both. Most of the casualties were from the mortar—which, fortunately, soon lifted and continued firing at the retreating landing craft. Two medical orderlies, who were brothers, remained with the wounded. One was taken prisoner with them; the other escorted three walking wounded along the cliff top to Beach One, two of whom were unfortunately killed on the way. One officer, leaving his boat, was hit by mortar fragments, his right hand becoming useless. Nevertheless he went on, and led a charge in the final assault on the battery, using his revolver and grenades with his left hand and accounting for a number of the enemy. He subsequently received a bar to his MC. A lance-corporal of R Signals was stunned by the same bomb. He recovered consciousness ten minutes later, and, knowing the plan and, as the only signaller in his section, knowing that he was of major importance, he pulled himself together and rejoined his section, by this time in the wood. He arrived in time to give Force HQ the necessary situation report before the assault signal. A private soldier, under heavy fire, climbed a telegraph pole and with his wirecutters cut lateral communications along the coast; he was awarded the MM.

As the troops were getting over the wire three Boston aircraft passed overhead and drew enemy fire from the commando who rushed to (23) and, crossing the Quiberville-St. Marguerite road, proceeded at the double along the east bank of the River Saane, in accordance with the plan. "B" Troop was in the lead, followed closely by Force HQ, then "F" Troop. Arrangements had been made to cover this advance with smoke if they were fired at from high ground near Quiberville. It was easy to keep direction below a steep bank that defiladed them from St. Marguerite and with the river on their right. The going, mostly through long grass, was heavy, since the river had overflowed its banks. The bend in the river where the force was to swing east was also easily identified, though by this time it was 0515 hours and broad daylight.

The ground from the river to the south-west corner of the wood (19) was more exposed though not devoid of cover. The more open spaces were crossed in open formation by bounds. By this time Group 2 could hear the heavy volume of small arms fire with which "C" Troop were engaging the battery, and soon afterwards the roar of the cordite explosion, and sheets of flames clearly visible above the trees, increased their confidence that all was going well.

On reaching the wood (19), "B" and "F" Troops divided according to plan and made their way towards their forming-up areas.

"B" Troop moved forward inside the southern edge of the wood and then filtered through the orchard by sub-sections. Using cover they approached the perimeter wire, where they came under inaccurate fire from a MG position, the flak tower (3), and from various buildings. From thereon they advanced by fire and movement with covering smoke. One MG was stalked and silenced with a grenade. They reached their assembly positions, just short of the main battery buildings, and reported at Z+95 that they were ready for the assault.

"F" Troop went through the wood to (15), from where they advanced under cover of smoke due north, on either side of the road, to the corner of the perimeter. Here a serjeant records that a number of Germans were surprised in a farmyard, while organizing a counter attack on "C" Troop. They were killed with Tommy guns. Vigorous opposition was encountered from the buildings and enclosures just inside the perimeter wire, and several casualties were sustained. The troop commander was killed by a stick grenade, and one of the section officers was mortally wounded. The serjeant took over but was also killed. The third officer was shot through the hand, the bullet lodging in his wrist, but he closed with his opponent and killed him. This officer took over command of the troop, and, in the final assault on the battery, though shot through the thigh, led his men in bayonet charges from one gun site to another. He was subsequently awarded the Victoria Cross. The troop serjeant-major was also badly wounded in the foot, but continued to engage the enemy in a sitting position; he received the DCM. Fighting their way forward and overcoming resistance, "F" Troop reached their start line under cover in a ditch along the road immediately behind the gun emplacements.

Force HQ consisting of the commander, adjutant, two runners, three signallers with No. 38 sets, and a protective section of four Tommy gunners from the Commando orderly room, had moved forward to the north-west corner of the wood, where a heartening situation report was received from the commander of Group 1. "A" Troop fighting patrol also reported that they were in a position west of the battery position about (17) and had inflicted heavy casualties. Force HQ now moved behind and between "B" and "F" Troops near the track junction (16), where the commander contacted officers commanding "B" and "F" Troops.

The time was now Z+95. During this move forward, being mistaken for the enemy, they came under heavy fire from a section of "F" Troop. RT was used to stop the fire.

At Z+90, exactly on time, a low-level cannon attack on the gun sites and battery position was made by a Hurricane squadron. This was only partly successful as the squadron came in mixed up with Focke-Wulfes.

The assault signal was given at about Z+100. "B" Troop rushed the buildings to the right of the gun sites, and "F" Troop the gun sites themselves. The charge of "F" Troop went in across open ground under fire, overrunning strong points, and finally ended on the gun sites themselves, where all the crews were bombed, shot, or bayoneted. "B" Troop had a somewhat easier task in the assault. Odd enemy groups were despatched in underground tunnels, in the battery office, in the cookhouse and outbuildings. Two German officers were killed after a rousing chase from one house to another. The guns, both barrels and breech blocks, instruments, and most of the subterranean stores and ammunition dumps, were blown up by "F" Troop. "B" Troop were responsible for mopping up and for all-round defence. The gun emplacements afterwards were a remarkable sight. Dead Germans were piled high up behind the sandbag breastworks which surround the guns. Many of them had been badly burned when the cordite had been set alight in the early stages of the operation. Other bodies of men who had been sniped by "C" and "A" Troops lay all round the area, in and out of bunkers, slit trenches, or buildings. Isolated resistance from pillboxes caused a further half dozen casualties, since all strong points were enfiladed from one section of the wire to another (the perimeter covered some 50 acres); when one position was stormed and the crews killed, the Commando personnel engaged came under heavy fire from the next position. Isolated snipers continued to resist from cover outside the gun emplacements. It was noted that they picked off single men moving by themselves but appeared unwilling to unmask their position during mopping up operations if two or more men exposed themselves simultaneously. Good use of smoke generators was made at this stage and the No. 77 Phosphorus Grenades, which explode on impact, proved particularly successful. Union Jacks for captured positions proved useful as recognition signals. The last survivors, like all the enemy encountered, fought well.

It may not be out of place to note that "CAULDRON" Force commander considers that the success of the operation was chiefly due to the excellence of junior leading and superior weapon training.

PART IV.—THE WITHDRAWAL

While the guns were being blown up, the force commander ordered the MO and stretcher bearers by RT to come up from the beach head to the battery position. "F" Troop, Force HQ, and "B" Troop, when the demolitions and mopping up were finished, moved successively down to Beach One, carrying their wounded and guided by elements of "C" Troop who were covering the withdrawal.

Meanwhile "A" Troop, acting as left flank guard, ambushed and shot up an enemy patrol coming from St. Marguerite. As an example of bad training, it is worthy of note that the enemy advanced points were too close together, and that the shot that sprang the ambush passed through the bodies of the two leading Germans.

It took some time to get the wounded through the wire, and time might have been saved had the gaps through it been widened while the operation was in progress. During the evacuation an enemy mortar began to shell the beach, but the 3-in. mortar, which had already been mounted on the beach to cover such an eventuality, judging its position by the line of flight of the approaching bombs returned the fire. This enemy mortar did not fire again. "C" Troop, forming the rear guard, were the last to withdraw, and did so in accordance with a frequently rehearsed drill whereby the LMGs in pairs leap-frogged one another, while the rear elements put up a smoke screen. Haversacks containing No. 18 smoke generators had been dumped for this purpose by the troop at the top of the gulley on their way up. The withdrawal across the rocks to the LCAs was made through a lane of smoke some 200 yards wide from No. 18 generators placed in position during the operation. The lane was extended for about 50 yards into the sea by naval smoke floats put out by the LCS and LCAs. When the LCAs were a few hundred yards out, and no longer under the lee of the cliffs, they came under inaccurate MG fire from the vicinity of the lighthouse, and further use was made of smoke until out of range.

Casualties

The total casualties of the operation were forty-five :—

Officers killed	2	Other ranks killed	10
Officers wounded	3	Other ranks wounded	17
		Other ranks wounded and missing	9
		Other ranks missing	4

No casualties were suffered during the withdrawal.

Of the 20 evacuated wounded, several had carried on right through the action. 12 of the 20 wounded were back at duty within two months.

CHAPTER 10

SMALL ARMS TRAINING,
VOLUME I, PAMPHLET NO.21
THE THOMPSON MACHINE CARBINE 1942

The War Office, 15 July 1942.

GENERAL NOTES

1. Object

The sole object of weapon training is to teach all ranks the most efficient way of handling their weapons in order to kill the enemy. Instructors will always bear this fact in mind and will continually impress it upon those whom they instruct.

2. *Safety precautions*

At the beginning of every lesson the instructor will inspect the machine carbine, pouches, and drill cartridges.

3. *Training*

Instructors must appreciate that, while the lessons are designed to be taught in one period, more time will be necessary in order to permit of sufficient practice to obtain proficiency.

Excellent training value can also be obtained by using the spotlight projector.

4. The machine carbine is normally the weapon of the section commander. Occasions will arise, however, when it may be advisable to give it to another man in the section.

Fig. 1

Weight Approx: 10 lb. Calibre: .450 in.

Carbines with vertical foregrips have the front swivel on the left side.

LESSON 1.—INTRODUCTION—LOADING AND UNLOADING

Instructor's Notes

Stores.—Machine carbine; magazines; drill cartridges, if available.

All parts will be named as dealt with (see Fig. 2).

1. Explain :—

The machine carbine is a short range weapon introduced for the purpose of engaging the enemy at ranges of from 10 to 100 yds. At greater distances the speed of the bullet is so reduced that it has lost much of its penetrative power.

The weapon is especially useful when on patrol, or for fighting in close country, such as woods and villages. It is ideal for use at night at very close ranges. If necessary it may be fired on the move during the assault. Under these conditions the enemy may appear at close ranges and from different directions, and by firing from the waist such targets can be instantly engaged. Where time permits the weapon should always be fired from the shoulder, as this method is far more accurate.

It is an automatic weapon, operated by the recoil of the spent case acting on the bolt face.

Fig. 2

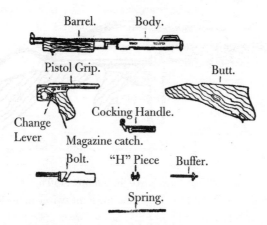

The machine carbine can be fired in bursts or in single rounds.

2. *Magazine filling*

    i. Explain and demonstrate :—

The magazine holds 20 rounds. Hold magazine in left hand, ribs away from the body. Pick up a convenient number of rounds in the right hand and place each round in by pressing downwards and backwards. Count the number of rounds, and ensure that ammunition is kept clean.

    ii. To empty—press each round forward with the nose of a bullet or remove with finger and thumb.

    iii. Practise squad.

3. *Loading and unloading*

Explain and demonstrate :—

    i. *To load.*—Hold the machine carbine with the right hand on the pistol grip, forefinger outside the trigger guard, butt under the arm, muzzle pointing down at an angle of 45 degrees. Turn the machine carbine to the right, grasp the magazine in the left hand, rib to the rear, and insert it in the recess in front of the trigger guard. Force the magazine upwards and ensure that it is FULLY ENGAGED.

Loading is fully completed by cocking the machine carbine when it is required to fire, or when action is imminent.

NOTE.—The safety catch should NEVER be used—it being only necessary to cock the weapon to be ready for firing.

ii. *To unload.*—Turn the machine carbine to the right. Press the magazine catch on the left side of the pistol grip upwards with the thumb of the left hand, and remove the magazine. Cock the machine carbine, if not already cocked, and, holding the cocking handle with the left hand, press the trigger and ease the working parts forward under control. Repeat this action.

iii. Practise   squad—Words   of   command—"Load"—"Action imminent"— "Unload".

4. *The sights*

Explain :—

The weapon is fitted with a simple fixed aperture battle sight, sighted for use at 100 yds. Rules for aiming as for L.M.G. With machine carbines not fitted with this battle sight, quick alignment can be made using the recess in the cocking handle.

LESSON 2.—HOLDING AND FIRING

Instructor's Notes

Stores.—Machine carbine; magazines; drill cartridges, if available; Fig. 2 target.

A magazine should be on the weapon when teaching holding.

Dress :—battle order.

1. *Holding*

i. Explain :—

Whether firing from the shoulder or the hip, holding is of the first importance. There is no shock of recoil when firing, but the weapon has a tendency to throw upwards when bursts are used. The individual can only find the exact hold required, to ensure hitting the enemy, by firing on the range.

ii. There are two positions for holding the weapon :—

(a) From the waist.

(b) From the shoulder.

2. i. Explain and demonstrate :—

      (*See* Fig. 3.)

      Holding from the waist.

The left foot is advanced with the knee bent, the weight of the body being balanced on the left foot. The right hand is on the pistol grip, with the forefinger on the trigger, the left hand on the foregrip. The butt of the weapon is pressed tightly against the side by the right arm. The left elbow is pulled well back into the body in such a way that, no matter in which direction the firer turns, the weapon is brought automatically in the same direction. The muzzle is directed towards the enemy, barrel horizontal. The attention of the firer must be concentrated on the target.

The position of the sling swivel as shown in Fig. 1 and *not* as above.

Fig. 3

ii. Practise squad, instructor standing behind man and checking that the barrel is aligned on the enemy.

3. i. Explain and demonstrate :—

      (See Fig. 4.)

Holding in the shoulder.

The position of the body and the hands is the same as when holding from the waist. The right elbow is raised and the right shoulder pushed well forward into the butt.

ii. Practise squad.

The postion of the sling swivel is as shown in Fig. 1 and not as above.

Fig. 4

4. *Firing*

i. Explain and demonstrate, where necessary :—

The machine carbine can be fired single rounds, by placing the change lever to the rear (this can only be done when the weapon is cocked), or in bursts by placing it forward. With experience, single rounds can be fired with the change lever at automatic, thus enabling it to be kept permanently in this position. Because of the speed with which single rounds can be fired, the greater accuracy obtained by this method, and the need for economy of ammunition, single-round firing should be employed whenever possible. Bursts should be reserved for extreme emergencies, and, when used, should be of two or three rounds only.

ii. The machine carbine can be carried in any convenient position, but when expecting to meet the enemy it should be held at the waist, supported by the sling round the neck.

iii. If time permits the weapon will always be fired from the shoulder, as this method is far more accurate. An approximate aim should be taken using the battle sight, if fitted, or the recess in the cocking handle. Should the enemy appear too suddenly to allow of this method being used, it should be fired from the waist by sense of direction. From this position it can be cocked and fired instantly. Whichever method is used an attempt should be made to observe the shots, as this is the only quick method of making necessary corrections. Although the weapon can be fired whilst on the move, greater accuracy is obtained by halting momentarily.

iv. Having disposed of the enemy the weapon can be placed at safety, to resume movement, by removing the magazine, easing the cocking handle forward, and placing on a full magazine.

5. *Immediate action*

Explain and demonstrate, using an empty magazine and also one fitted with a depressor, if drill cartridges are not available :—

(A halfpenny makes a good depressor.)

i. When the magazine becomes empty the machine carbine will stop with the cocking handle to the rear. The remedy is to change the magazine and continue firing.

ii. If the machine carbine stops during firing, cock it and continue firing.

iii. Should the above immediate action fail, then cock the machine carbine, turn it to the right, and shake vigorously, when a live round or an empty case should fall out; continue firing.

iv. If nothing falls out when the machine carbine is shaken, remove the magazine, when the obstruction should drop out. Look into the chamber, if practicable, replace magazine (or a full one) and continue firing.

NOTE.—Unless drill cartridges are available, working parts must be eased forward under control to prevent damage.

v. Practise squad, varying the order of stoppages as progress is made.

INDEX

A.A. discipline 64–65

All-in Fighting 28–40
  No.12. Thumb Hold 28–30, 29, 30
  No.13. Sentry Hold 31–33, 31, 32, 33
  No.14. Japanese strangle 34–35, 34, 35
  No.14(A). Japanese strangle applied from in front 36, 36
  No.15. Handcuff hold 37–38, 37, 38
  No.16. Bent arm hold 38–39, 39
  No.17. Head hold 40, 40

Bayonet practice 20–21
Beach, the 63
Bivouac, the 77–78
Boat drill 63
Bridges, demolition of 22–24, 26–27

Casualty evacuation 64
Co-operation between the Services 62–63
Combined Operations Pamphlet No. 24 Cliff Assaults 89–100
  Section 7 – Cliff Climbing Methods and Drills 89–99
    Assault wave climbing equipment 90
    Assault wave organization 90
    Casualty evacuation 97–
    Cliff withdrawals 99
    Climbing personnel within the follow-up troops 95–96
    Day or night assault drill 91, 92, 93, 94
    Follow-up wave – link up with the initial assault 95
    Formation of assault bridgehead at night 94–95
    General considerations 89
    Heavily laden personnel 97
    Heavy stores 97
    Reorganization of the follow-up troops at the cliff top 96–97
    Signals on the bridgehead 91
  Appendix D: Diagrammatic Layout of a Cliff Bridgehead Showing the Position of Guiding Tapes 100
Combined Operations Pamphlet No. 27: Hardening of Commando Troops for Warfare 67–88
  Foreword 67
  Chapter 1: The Hardening of the Body
    Section 1 – General 67–68
    Section 2 – Resistance to Exposure 68–71
    Section 3 – Resistance to Fatigue 71–73
    Section 4 – Procedure during Training 73–74
    Section 5 – Staleness 74–77
  Chapter 3: The Bivouac
    Section 11 - Sleeping and Cooking in the Open 77–78
  Chapter 4: Seasickness and Immersion in Water
    Section 12 – Prevention of Seasickness 78–79
    Section 18 – Immersion in Water and Spray 79–80
  Chapter 5: The Science of Rationing
    Section 14 – Food 80–84
    Section 15 – Vitamins 84–87
    Section 16 – Condensed Rations 87–88

Commando Training 51–66
  I. General
    1. Role and organization require settlement 51–52
    2. Offensive spirit. Training at night 52
    3. Initial Troubles 52
    4. Lack of supporting weapons and administrative organization 52
    5. Role limited to raids 52
    6. Premium placed on discipline 52–53
    7. The problem of specialists 53
    8. Sappers and signallers essential 53
    9. "Amateur" Sappers unsuccessful 54
    10. All ranks trained in S/P and morse 54
    11. Progressive training 55–56
  II. Individual Training
    12. T.O.E.T. 56
    13. Eradication of the unfit 56
    14. Familiarity with the elements 56–57
    15. Self-confidence and initiative: various subjects 57–58
    16. Training by night all-important 58–59
  III. Collective Training
    17. Inter-Unit Schemes 59
    18. Control 59
    19. Protection 59
    20. Interference with Junior Leaders 60
    21. Dress and equipment 60
    22. Further miscellaneous subjects 60
    23. Speed essential 60–61
    24. Obstacles: Wire 61
    25. Formations 61
    26. Recognition 61–62
    27. Mountain Climbing: Sabotage 62
  IV. Inter-service Training
    28. Co-operation between the Services 62–63
    29. Accommodation in H.M. Ships 63
    30. Early lessons: Boat Drill 63
    31. The Beach 63
    32. Withdrawal and Re-embarkation 63–64
    33. Evacuation of casualties 64
    34. A.A. discipline 64–65
    35. Later stages of training 65–66
    36. Conclusion 66
Commando Training Instruction No.1 16–19
  aim of training 16–17
  collective training 19
  individual training 17–18

Dieppe Raid 101–18
Discipline 52–53
Dress and equipment 60

Fighting, All-in 28–40
Food 80–84

Hardening of the Body 67–77

Inter-Unit Schemes 59

Lock gates, demolition of 25

Morse 54
Mountain climbing: sabotage 62

Night training 52, 58–59

Notes from Theatres of War No.11
  Destruction of a Germany Battery
  by No.4 Commando during the
  Dieppe Raid 101–18
  Operation "Cauldron"
  Varengeville 19th August, 1942
  Introduction 102–5
  Part I – The Problem 105–7, 106
  Part II – The Plan 107–10
  Part III – The Narrative 110–17
  Part IV – The Withdrawal 117–18

Notes on Training of Commandos:
  Weapon Training: Bayonet 20–21

Offensive Demolitions 22–27
  Lecture 4: the scope of explosives
  22–26
    1. Quick destruction 22
    2. Bridges 22–24
    3. Roads 24
    4. Railways 25
    5. Lock Gates 25
    6. Other demolitions 25
    7. Organisations 25
    8. Strategy 25
  Practical 4: Placing Charges 26–27

Raiding operations, stages of 19
Railways, demolition of 25
Rations, condensed 87–88
Roads, demolition of 24

S/P 54
Sappers 53, 54
Seasickness, prevention of 78–79
Ships, accommodation on 63
Shooting to Live with the One-hand
  Gun 41–50
  Chapter IV Training: Advanced

Methods
  "Three-quarter Hip" Position 41–
  42, 44
  Front View 48, 49, 49
  "Half Hip" Position 45–46, 45
  ☒"Quarter" or "Close-Hip"
  Position 46, 46
  Side View 48–49, 48
  Two-Handed, Prone 47–48, 48
  Two-Handed, Standing 47, 47
  use of sights 49–50

Signallers 53

Small Arms Training, Volume I,
  Pamphlet No.21: The Thompson
  Machine Carbine 1942
  General Notes 119, 120
  Lesson 1 – Introduction - Loading
  and Unloading 120–22, 121
  Lesson 2 – Holding and Firing
  122–25, 123, 124

Vitamins 84–87

Water and spray, immersion in 79–80
Wire obstacles 61
Withdrawal and re-embarkation 63–
  64